MY LIFE
FROM NORMANDY
TO HOCKEYTOWN

My Life: From Normandy to Hockeytown

Copyright © 2007 Olympia Entertainment Inc.

Executive Editor: Michael Bayoff

Managing Editor: Bill Roose

Editorial: Bob Duff

Copy editors: Michael Passman, Bill Roose

Layout & Design: Craig C. Wheeler

Cover design: Bill Roose

Produced by: CFW Creative Sports, Inc.

LIBRARY of CONGRESS CONTROL NUMBER: 2007934838

ISBN: 0-9664120-8-7
ISBN 13: 9780966412086

Printed in the United States

Other recent books by Olympia Entertainment:
• *Nine: A Salute to Mr. Hockey, Gordie Howe*
• *Nineteen: A Salute to Steve Yzerman*
• *The ABCs of Detroit Red Wings Hockey*

To order, call 1-800-WINGS-25

"Best Wishes"

I dedicate this book to the late Detroit Red Wings GM Jack Adams, who recommended me to cover the team in 1949; to Mike and Marian Ilitch, who kept me at the Red Wings' microphone for this long and enjoyable career, and to the women in my life - my mother, Margaret Lynch, my sisters Margaret and Edith, my deceased wives Fran and Thelma, the Canadian nurses overseas during World War II, my daughters Janis, Valerie, Mary, Francey, Patricia and Lori and to my continuing companionship with Nancy

Sincerely,

Budd Lynch

RED WINGS   SINCE 1949

NHL HALL OF FAME   1985

MICHIGAN HALL OF FAME
1994

BUDD LYNCH
A RED WINGS INSTITUTION

Dear Hockey Fans,

Budd Lynch is as much a part of Hockeytown as the Red Wings and Detroit hockey fans. As he enters his 59th season with the Red Wings organization, Budd has the distinction of being the person with the longest association with the team. His career began in 1949 as the Red Wings' game broadcaster – first on radio and then on television. When he attempted retirement in 1975, Alex Delvecchio convinced him to head the public relations department. He again tried to retire 10 years later, but we could not let this great ambassador for our team leave. We offered him the position of Red Wings PA announcer and are delighted he accepted. His great voice is known throughout the NHL and he is well respected throughout the world of sports.

During his illustrious career with the Red Wings, Budd has worked with four owners, 10 general managers and 25 coaches. He has experienced the glory years, the lean years, the rebuilding years, and championship years of the team. He has worked with the giants of the game but also has developed a rapport with the fans that has endeared him to generations of Detroiters.

As you read the story of Budd's life "From Normandy to Hockeytown" we are confident you will grow to love the man as much as we do. You will admire how he has faced the challenges in his life, enjoy his sense of humor and admire his caring heart. Budd Lunch is a Red Wings institution! And we are so proud and thankful that he is.

Mike and Marian Ilitch
Owners, Detroit Red Wings

CONTENTS

Foreword

I've been asked to write a brief preface to this book about Budd . . . for Pete's sake, I guess I could write the whole book and still have a bundle of material left over.

Our friendship started back in 1950. Budd's beloved Red Wings had their training camp in Sault Ste. Marie, Mich. I was a young and very green announcer in the local radio station and thrilled to be anywhere close to the Red Wings. The general manager, Jack Adams and the publicist, Fred Huber, became friends of mine, but it was Budd Lynch who took all sorts of time to introduce me to the world of big-league hockey.

A few years later, I accepted a job at a local radio station in Pontiac. You could imagine how exciting it was for me when Budd came walking into the little station with Adams in tow. Interviewing one of Detroit's most popular sports figures impressed the powers-that-be at the station and raised my status in their thinking. Budd had gone out of his way to help.

Some nine or 10 years later, the Stroh Brewery called and asked if I would be interested in broadcasting the Wings games. I would be working alongside Budd. It was something I'd dreamed about for years, but I entered the situation with some trepidation. After all his years of being the "voice" of the Red Wings, how would he feel about a newcomer moving into the picture? Well, let me tell you, as I've often said, this one-armed bandit welcomed me with "open arm." It didn't take long to find out how respected and well-liked he was in every NHL city we visited. And rather than going his own way, he made a point of introducing me to his friends, fellow announcers, team officials and anyone else who could be helpful to our broadcasts.

Ours was a relationship that continued in and out of the broadcast booth. When we traveled on the hundred or so road trips, we ate together, drank a little together and the son of a gun even got me onto cigars, which we smoked together. And through it all, we talked a lot. Budd's conversations would always include his six daughters, of whom he was justifiably proud. Through the years, I've met them and got to know them and can understand why he loves them so much. Budd's wife Thelma and my wife Donna were close and were social friends for years. When Thelma passed away, we shared Budd's grief.

During the course of this book, you'll read of Budd's military career. It resulted in not only the loss of his right arm, but the shoulder as well. One would think that this would handicap a person for life. But not this person. He soon shunned any prothesis and made the most of his left side. To tell you the truth, there wasn't much of anything he couldn't do and do well. If a waiter offered to cut his steak, he'd face a withering look and was told by Budd if he couldn't cut it, it was going back to the kitchen (which never happened).

I can only recall one time during which he was maybe stymied. The Wings had played poorly and lost an away game and the mood on the bus to the airport was tense. The bus was dark and quiet. Then a voice came from the back of the seats. It was team captain Alex Delvecchio, "Budd, we've got a question for you," Delvecchio said. So Budd reached down to grab the records he kept on the team to give Delvecchio an answer, as Delvecchio continued his question. "Budd," he said, "How in hell do you wind your watch?" I can't remember any answer from Budd, but he laughed and laughed and the solemn ride brightened up considerably.

That's Budd in a nutshell. He's brightened up a lot of lives. He has made hundreds of unannounced and unpublicized visits to encourage and otherwise help new amputees. And it must go without question that he has been a great inspiration to others with handicaps, though I'm here to tell you that Mr. Lynch never considered himself handicapped in any way.

On the subject of handicaps, it's always fun to play golf with Budd, which we've done often. He plays with righthanded clubs, swinging through the ball with his left arm and playing a great game. Although, I sometimes question his scorekeeping, pointing out that he often seems incapable of counting past five, the number of his fingers. If you've never played golf with Budd, you've missed a great experience. As a matter of fact, if you've never had the opportunity to meet him, I hope this book will bring you closer to this great guy.

So, I guess you could surmise from all of this that one of the great things in my life has been my close friendship with one of the nicest, fun-loving and all-around great guys . . . Budd Lynch.

Enjoy the book.

Bruce Martyn

Introduction

The parade is never ending. One by one, the fans make the trek to the upper reaches of Joe Louis Arena, with a simple task in mind - to make the acquaintance of Budd Lynch.

It is always a trip worth every step of the journey.

A smile, a handshake, some friendly banter and an autograph later, they leave with the knowledge that they've met a true Detroit Red Wings legend, someone whose legacy within the organization's rich history belongs right up there alongside Gordie Howe and Steve Yzerman.

When Lynch made his NHL debut, Howe was a mere 21 years of age, still a relative newcomer to the hockey world, with just three years of NHL experience under his belt.

Twenty-two years later, when Howe hung them up for the first time, Lynch, who saw Mr. Hockey play more than anyone, was still calling the play-by-play of Detroit games.

Yzerman wasn't even born until the spring of 1965, shortly after Lynch had finished describing a first-place finish by the Red Wings during the 1964-65 season. The next time the Wings finished first overall in the standings, in 1995, Yzerman was an integral part of the Wings and so was Lynch, who'd moved into the role of JLA public address announcer, his dulcet, baritone voice delivering each goal announcement with steadiness and professionalism, leaving the hyperbole to others.

Beyond the boundless charm, the ever-present upbeat mood, the glimmering smile and the endless supply of jokes from his famous self-deprecating sense of humor, Lynch never hides his own belief that he has lived a blessed life.

He's worked alongside the legends of hockey, from Jack Adams and Lester Patrick to Sid Abel and Scotty Bowman and shares their Hall of Fame status. A true pioneer of the game, for a generation of Red Wings fans, in the days before satellites beamed every game into their living rooms, Lynch was the people's connection to Red Wings hockey, his voice describing in vivid imagery every one of Ted Lindsay's punishing checks, Red Kelly's rink-length rushes and Roger Crozier's acrobatic saves.

Cite a magical moment in Red Wings history and it's more than likely that Lynch was there. He was at the mic when Pete Babando tallied in double overtime to win the 1950 Stanley Cup. He detailed every stop as

Terry Sawchuk posted a record four shutouts in the 1952 finals. He was there the night that the first octopus rained down from the seats onto the ice surface at Olympia Stadium. He called the goal the night Howe surpassed Maurice (Rocket) Richard to become the NHL's leading goal scorer.

He was on the job the night Montreal fans protested the Rocket's suspension, leading to the Richard Riot the night of March 17, 1955. The Wings won their fourth Cup in six years that spring and although they waited 52 years to lift Lord Stanley's mug again, the ever-present Lynch was left with the honor of calling Darren McCarty's Cup-winning goal against Philadelphia to the delight of a raucous, sold-out JLA crowd.

He's witnessed, in-person, the Production Line, the Bruise Brothers, the Grind Line and the Russian Five. He was there when the Ilitch family brought the Dead Wings back to life and for Yzerman's entire reign as hockey's longest-serving captain.

Originally hired by Adams in the fall of 1949, Lynch was instrumental in the introduction of the Jack Adams Trophy, which is presented annually to the NHL's coach of the year.

His hockey career alone is one worthy of legendary status, but it's only one chapter of Lynch's amazing story. He did play-by-play of junior games in his hometown of Windsor, seeing the likes of future Hall of Famers like Sawchuk, Howe and Marcel Pronovost in action before they'd ever turned pro. On the gridiron, he called the action for the NFL's Detroit Lions and also for college football games involving Michigan, Michigan State and Notre Dame. He even did a stint as a ring announcer for professional wrestling.

Long before his voice made him a household name, Lynch was among the thousands of brave, faceless men who put their lives on the line for freedom, fighting for the Allies in World War II. A member of the Canadian Army's Essex Scottish regiment, Lynch landed on the beaches of Normandy, France on D-Day and nearly made the ultimate sacrifice for his country in battle, losing his right arm and shoulder when hit by a German shell in Caen, France, in the summer of 1944.

Instead of feeling sorry for himself, Lynch was already working in radio before he enlisted, deployed his vocal chords to continue to contribute to the war effort. He worked for the BBC's Armed Forces Expeditionary Forces Program as an on-air personality and producer. He produced shows for the famous American bandleader Glenn Miller and Lynch's work on his own show "Combat Diary" earned him citations from both British Prime

Minister Winston Churchill and Allied forces leader General Dwight D. Eisenhower.

A member of the War Amps of Canada, Lynch never turns down a request from someone whose life has been affected by the loss of a limb, willingly offering assistance, advice and a friendly ear to listen. He's never viewed the loss of his arm as a handicap and actually boasts that his one-armed golf game is far superior to his performance as a two-hander.

Perhaps it's fitting that Lynch's perch on game night is high above the ice surface, up near the rafters where banners honoring Detroit's retired sweater numbers hang in a place of honor.

Howe . . . Lindsay . . . Abel . . . Sawchuk . . . Delvecchio . . . Yzerman . . . Lynch.

Every one of them, Red Wings legends in their own unique way.

Bob Duff
September 2007

A Budd Blossoms

CHAPTER ONE

❝ *We've got too many Franks . . . let's make it Len, Larry, or Tom."*

**-Radio station manager,
CHML, Hamilton, Ontario**

Whenever I meet people, everybody asks the same question - "Why two Ds in Budd? There must be a story behind it."

As a matter of fact, there is. Quite a story, to tell the truth.

In high school at Cathedral High in Hamilton, Ont., I was Frank Joseph James Lynch. It turned out that in the summer of 1937, I took a crazy chance. They were holding auditions for part-time work at the radio station in Hamilton, CHML. Well, I guess I must have impressed someone, because I got called a couple of days later and they wanted me to go to work for Percy LeSueur, who ran the sports department at the station.

LeSueur was quite the famous name in Canada. He was a Hall of Fame goalie way back when, who played for the mighty Ottawa Silver Seven, winning three Stanley Cups. Legend has it he used the same goal stick for six straight seasons between 1906-10.

LeSueur even had ties to this area. He was the first manager of the Windsor Arena and Detroit's Olympia Stadium and the first coach of the Detroit Olympics, who were the original farm team for the Red Wings organization. So hockey was starting in my life right then.

The next day, when I came in and was told I had the job, the manager of the radio station said, "We've got too many Franks at the station, so let's make it Len, or Larry, or Tom." So I said, "Let me think about it and when I come in tomorrow, I'll have a name for you."

Well, my mother loved Laura Secord chocolate candy bud drops. Walking home that night, I went and got some chocolate buds for her. And I thought, "I'm going to make my name Bud and I'm going to put another D on it." And that's what I did. I went in the next day and told the manager, "My name is going to be Budd with two Ds." That's the way it started.

In the army, it was always Budd first with two Ds. When I came over to the United States and became an American citizen, I had it legally changed to Budd J.J. Lynch.

But we're getting ahead of ourselves in the story. This Budd still had to bloom.

My mom and dad, Jim and Margaret Lynch, were married in Hamilton. My father was head of the freight division for Canada Steamship Lines, and his job required that he move around a lot. He'd been assigned to Windsor, Ont. shortly before I was born.

I came into the world in Windsor on Aug. 7, 1917, the oldest and the only son among what would be three children. I was born at Vine and Pellissier because my mother couldn't get to Hotel Dieu Hospital, which was one block away. I've shown my kids the house where I was born and they'd say, "What do you mean you were born there? The hospital is right over there." I guess I was someone who liked to arrive on schedule. I wanted to show up on time, so they didn't get to the hospital.

I traveled quite extensively as a kid. Our family was always on the go. I was in Windsor and then my dad got sent to Chicago, so we moved there when I was still quite young. In 1919, he went to Toronto and then back to Montreal and got another promotion. My sister Marg was born in Montreal. By that time, my father was working in the head office for Canada Steamship Lines, but tragedy was about to strike the world and right within the Lynch household.

World War I, or the Great War, as it was known in those days, had just ended with Germany's surrender on Nov. 11, 1918, and shortly after the severe flu epidemic hit that killed millions of people all over the world.

That flu epidemic ravaged the planet. It was known as the Spanish influenza epidemic because so many people died from the illness in Spain, but research shows that no one was ever certain of the pandemic's origins.

Estimates are that one-quarter of the people in the United States and a fifth of the world's population were infected with the virus. Some 200,000 were killed in the month of October 1918 alone, including Hamby Shore, a defenseman with the National Hockey League's Ottawa Senators. The disease became so rampant that during the 1919 Stanley Cup final, so many Montreal Canadiens players were bedridden with flu that the series had to be halted. The Seattle Metropolitans were offered the trophy by default but declined to accept the Cup, feeling it wouldn't have been right to win in such manner. Shortly after, Montreal defenseman Joe Hall, hospitalized in Seattle, died from the disease.

Hospital facilities, already taxed to the limits by wounded war veterans returning home, weren't prepared to deal with such an onslaught of sickness. Such was the carnage that there was a shortage of gravediggers and coffins to bury victims. My mother used to tell us that they couldn't bury any of the bodies because they were afraid of contamination, so they'd have 500 piled up here and a thousand piled up there on the outskirts of Montreal for two weeks before they could even bury them. They took a lot of the bodies to Hamilton to bury them.

History studies suggest that between 50 and 100 million people were killed by the disease in a one-year span. What made this strain of influenza even more puzzling was that it struck down many people in the prime of their life. One of those unfortunate souls was my father James Lynch. He took sick with the flu and it turned out that he passed away.

I was only two-and-a-half years old when my father died. My sister Marg was just a year old at the time. Mom was expecting, so we moved back to Hamilton, which was where she came from. My sister Edie was born in Hamilton. Mom raised the three of us little brats. That's where we went to school, in Hamilton. I never got beyond high school, unfortunately, and I made sure every one of my kids got college educations. That was the one thing I emphasized with them. I never went to college, I didn't have time to, with no dad and being a fund raiser for the family, so I made sure that they did. I have no regrets about it, but it's always part of life. I told all the girls, whatever you want to be, nurse, doctor, lawyer, technician, cosmetologist, whatever, you've got to have an education. They all agreed that it was a great thrill to go to college.

After my father's death, I promised to put my two sisters through school. One wanted to be a nurse and one wanted to get into cosmetics. Edith became a nurse. She trained at St Joseph's Hospital in Hamilton and even trained in Detroit for awhile. She had seven children. Marg, my other sister, she had one child. They both used to kid me, "Why did you go overseas to fight in World War II? You cheapskate, you weren't here for either of our weddings."

Back then, when we were growing up, I worked all the time. In high school, I worked part-time at a drug store, and I worked part-time at a hardware store. My mother was still working at the time for the Right House, which was a big household store.

I wanted to follow in my father's footsteps, so the first two years in high school, I had worked on the boats in the summertime. I applied to Canada Steamship Lines and I worked as a deckhand. What an experience that was.

I worked on the freighters. On our ship, there was a coal carrier and you had to go down and shovel coal. You'd shovel for 20 minutes, come back up for 40, then back in for another 20. The old timers, the core of the ship, the guys in charge of keeping the fire pot going as they used to say, they'd drink buttermilk, so that the heat didn't bother them. They insisted I try it. Well, I'll tell you, I was sicker than a dog that first time.

The next year, I became a bellhop on the passenger boats from Toronto to Montreal. Paul Kidd, a guy who actually later became a lawyer and then was vice-president of Hiram Walker in Windsor, was our senior bell captain. All he kept saying was, "It's four-and-a-half months work, you get two shore leaves and you better have a bank account, because you're not spending any money." I saved an awful lot of money that summer.

Paul used to be stubborn. I'd say, "I'm a Catholic and I've got to get off the ship for Sunday morning Mass," but he never bought it. "There's a priest on board," he'd answer. "He'll bless you. You're not getting off." I later learned from talking to some of the other boys that Paul's dad was a minister in Kingston, Ontario. So when we got into Kingston, I said, "Paul, you're grounded. You can't go ashore. I'll go ashore and see your dad." "What do you know about my dad?" he demanded to know.

By the way, there's something you should know about us Lynches. The Lynch name is famous, or infamous, one or the other, depending upon how you look at it. Thomas Lynch is the youngest signatory on the American Declaration of Independence. The name Lynch was spelled different ways - Linch, Lynch - and there were different tribes all over Ireland. But away back in 1493, the mayor of Galway, Ireland was James Lynch. As I mentioned earlier, my dad's name was James Lynch as well. This other James Lynch, the one from Galway, he was in charge of the town's judiciary on top of being the mayor and he was left to deal with a difficult case, perhaps the toughest adjudication in history.

His own son, Walter Lynch, had stabbed a boy that was visiting from Spain and killed the kid. And James Lynch, in his duties as judge, found Walter Lynch guilty of murder and he said his son had to be hung. The mayor, again who was James Lynch, ordered the hanging in front of the city hall. When no one could be found who was willing to carry out the sentence, legend has it that James Lynch hung his own son. And then he quit politics and disappeared into seclusion for the remainder of his days.

The theory is that's where the original term of lynching started. Two of the women I knew who worked at Joe Louis Arena were visiting Galway and on top of a bank, there was a plaque, "Son was condemned by the mayor of this city, Lynch." It's called the Lynch Memorial and it is situated near the church of St. Nicholas in the form of a black marble stone over a built-up Gothic doorway.

I want to go back to Ireland one more time to study up on the family history some more, maybe even visit the Lynch Memorial, but it's not an easy task to tour the homeland. You go from bar to bar and castle to castle. You've got to train for that, I think.

Being a member of the Lynch clan in Hamilton was challenging, but I'll never forget how hard my mom worked to raise the three of us on her own and the sacrifices she made. Times were tough and like everything else, we had no car. Bicycles were our method of transportation. In Hamilton, the houses were so close together, you were lucky to get a bicycle between them. You walked everywhere, or you rode your bike.

We played all kinds of sports as kids - hockey, baseball, football, lacrosse. I played juvenile hockey in Hamilton and we used to scrimmage against the mighty Hamilton Tigers senior team. What a lineup they had - Goney McGowan, Maxie Bennett, the legendary Hector (Toe) Blake, who later won a total of 11 Stanley Cups as a player and coach with the Montreal Canadiens and the great Syl Apps, who was the big star from McMaster University. He hadn't turned pro yet, but he would captain the Toronto Maple Leafs to three Stanley Cups.

We also tried a sport that would certainly be considered outside the mainstream by most people. In high school, we rowed at the Leander Boat Club. I was in the fours down on Burlington Bay. One year, we went down to Port Dalhousie for the big sculling regatta. We didn't win, but it was quite a thrill. Bobby Pearce was our coach. He came from Australia and he was a big bruiser. He used to tongue lash us. "OK, you guys think you're lacrosse players, you think you're football players, you think you're baseball players? Well, this is a different sport. The four of you guys work together or I'll throw you in the water." Well, we took one look at dirty Burlington Bay and didn't like that idea at all. But it was fun, a different type of an education. I was No. 2 in the boat. Having a coxswain in a boat in those days was very, very rare. They put them in the eights eventually, but everything was controlled by No. 4 in our boat. Nos. 1, 2 and 3 had to know they were going in the right direction and it was up to the fourth rower in the boat to make sure of that.

You don't see that kind of variety in the athletic pursuits of children these days. The kids today, they specialize in sports at the high-school level. We never did. We played lacrosse, we played baseball, we played hockey as well. We used to put our skates on the linoleum floor in your own kitchen and go out and skate maybe three-quarters of a mile down to Scott's Park to an outdoor rink. Today, everything's made for the kids. It's all so structured.

By the time high school was winding down for me, I was thinking about structure in my life, about finding a career to pursue. I didn't have anything set in mind and the radio gig just kind of came up on a lark. At the time, I never expected that it would become my life's work. But it just goes to show that you never know what fate has in store for you.

Over The Airwaves And Overseas

CHAPTER TWO

" *I always believed if I could walk and talk, then I would live."*

- Budd Lynch

Entering the radio game was an entirely new world to me. I began as a staff announcer at CHML in Hamilton in 1936 and a year later, moved into news and sports at CKOC, another Hamilton station, where I did my first play-by-play work, learning the ropes from Percy LeSueur.

Percy LeSueur, he was up in years then, but he was a great goalkeeper in his day, a member of the Hockey Hall of Fame. He became the coach of Hamilton's NHL team in the 1920s and later went into first the newspaper business and then radio. Percy had a son named Steve Douglas who was very famous in broadcasting, too.

That first year, I had a chance to work the senior hockey games with Percy at Hamilton's Barton Street Arena. It was kind of interesting, because the Hamilton Tigers had quite a powerful squad, lining up future Hall of Famers such as Toe Blake and Syl Apps.

The following spring, the station got the contract to do PONY League baseball. So I worked with Percy LeSueur doing PONY League baseball in Hamilton. The St. Louis Cardinals were the parent club for the Hamilton team. The league's name stood for Pennsylvania, Ontario and New York. You traveled from Hamilton to London, to Batavia, New York, to Olean, New York, to Erie, Pennsylvania. It was a great experience for a young kid in high school.

When I got into radio, the bug was biting me. I guess it was learning from other people that got me so fired up about the business. Percy LeSueur worked on the Hot Stove Lounge broadcasts during Toronto Maple Leafs games at Maple Leaf Gardens, so he took me to Toronto for a Maple Leafs game one time when I was in high school and it happened to be Detroit and Toronto that were playing.

That's when I was introduced to Foster Hewitt. Percy LeSueur had all kinds of contacts with Imperial Oil. They were the ones who sponsored "Hockey Night in Canada". It was quite a thrill going into Maple Leaf Gardens. You were awed, first of all, by the pictures on the wall. On that particular day, they had the pipe band playing, the brass band. Saturday night, it was "Hockey Night in Canada" more so because they had entertainment there. I got to know Leafs owner Connie Smythe overseas during the war years. He was a major in the Canadian forces with the artillery, and I was with the Essex Scottish. In his own way, Connie was an ornery, tough guy. He decided to bring in the military bands to play at the Toronto games. At the one end of Maple Leaf Gardens, Saturday nights only, there'd be about 40 seats filled with pipers and brass bands. It was great entertainment. After a while, they decided to play canned music so they could sell another 40 seats and get rid of the freeloaders with the instruments.

Years earlier, when I was just a young lad, Hamilton had its own NHL team. I heard about them, but never got to see them play in person. The people who owned the Barton Street Arena were part of the operation that ran the team. After the NHL left in 1925, the city had a minor pro club, but as the years went on, there was no way they could have a real pro team anymore. The arena just wasn't suitable.

In 1939, I came down to Windsor, my birthplace, with Cam Ritchie, a radio guy I worked with from Hamilton, to work at CKLW. Ted Campeau, the president of CKLW, brought us down. It was a big break for me, because I also got to work with the Mutual Network, which owned CKLW at the time.

When I came to Windsor in 1939 from Hamilton, little did I think my first assignment would be doing a Gold Cup race.

When I was in Hamilton, on Burlington Bay, I had gotten to know a Commodore Greening, who owned a powerboat, a little racing boat. I had learned a little bit about powerboats and rooster tails. I had all the word knowledge, I just had to describe what I was seeing. The rooster tail, that's what sprays off the back end of the boat when it's racing.

I was given the assignment to be the backup to Joe Gentile on the boat races at the Detroit Yacht Club. The races had be delayed because of bad weather and at 4:45 p.m., Joe was nowhere to be found and we were 15 minutes before the start of the Gold Cup. They said, "You're on" and my introduction was, "Welcome to the Gold Cup on the Detroit River from the Detroit Yacht Club. The heats that were SHED-uled for earlier today have been canceled. But there is a heat that is going to take place right now." Well, the engineer grabbed me by the arm, pulled me over and said, "We're on a SKED-ule, you idiot." That was my introduction to international language. I had used the Canadian version of the word.

The water was choppy that day and I remember that Tempo 5, with

Guy Lombardo at the wheel, washed out right in front of me, so I wasn't the only one having a rough time of it.

We had ourselves a lot of great times in those days. We'd go over at three in the morning to play hockey at Windsor Arena. There'd be guys from the newspaper and guys from the wire services who were ex-Canadians. I think they charged us $30 for an hour. The ice had been cut up by three other teams before you'd get on. There was no resurfacing in those days. But it was fun. Then I'd have to go to work on three hours sleep. The crazy things you do when you're young.

It was September of 1939 when I first came to Windsor and war had been declared by the British Empire, so that fall, Cam and I decided to join the Essex Scottish Second Battalion reserves. You sort of felt that you wanted to volunteer. I was single and I figured, "I don't want to be called as part of a conscription." The government had talked about doing that, but they wanted volunteers.

We joined the second battalion. We used to parade every Friday night up and down Ouellette Avenue, right in the heart of downtown Windsor. One thing about joining the Essex Scottish: the bagpipes, they made you walk at a different pace. Then the brass band, they woke you up.

We went to training camp, the officers school, in London, Ontario and under canvas, three of us got pneumonia. I got out of there and survived. By the time we came back, the war had really started to develop then. There was the tragedy of Dieppe, when the Essex Scottish No. 1 Battalion had gone overseas and they were wiped out, about 70 percent of the soldiers either ending up prisoners of war or killed. They couldn't get the troops out. They never thought to have rescue parties to bring them off the shore.

One wonderful thing I did before heading overseas. Francis Gee, the women I'd met in Hamilton and fallen in love with, accepted my proposal. We got married just before I went overseas.

We decided to go on active duty, and they sent Cam and I to officers school in Brockville, Ontario. From there, when we graduated, we were reserve officers, so we hadn't been called to active duty overseas yet. We got sent -- of all places -- to Niagara-on-the-Lake, which is right by Niagara Falls. They were assembling a troop train to go to Prince George, British Columbia, and they made me the adjutant. There were 348 personnel, some

Nice legs. That's me in the kilt alongside fellow Essex Scottish solider Art Carley.

A man and his motorcycle. Getting ready to go for a ride in England. 1943.

I find this photo very ironic. For some reason, I posed at the Aldershot, England barracks with my right arm behind my back in April 1944, a few months before losing the arm in combat.

Major Budd Lynch of the Essex Scottish Unit, serving working for BBC radio in 1944.

senior officers, a captain and a couple of colonels and we had to stop in just about every city all across Canada to parade up and down and let the people know that we were the volunteers.

Then we went to Prince George, British Columbia, because the government thought the Japanese were setting fire to British Columbia with incendiary bombs. They've had those Mother Nature fires in British Columbia for years. They're called forest fires. You might have heard of them.

Anyway, we get out there and it was another experience because none of us knew anything about that kind of camping life - tear down some trees, put up a tent. There were guys from London, Ontario, guys from Chatham, Ontario. We experienced that for about the better part of four weeks, then we got the urgent call to report back to Windsor to be sent over to reinforce the Essex Scottish in England. So we went back to Hamilton, then to Debert, Nova Scotia. We were on a converted banana schooner going across the ocean. There were doctors, a few Red Cross volunteers, some nurses and 120 of us young punks and two Beaufort guns that were the armored part of this banana schooner, but one of them didn't work.

We'd never fired a Beaufort gun before, so we all had to practice. We were on the ocean 21 days all told, from Debert, Nova Scotia, along the coastline almost to Boston, and then back up through the gulf to Labrador, to Iceland, to Greenland, to Ireland, then to Cardiff, Wales, where we landed. We found out later that we were the armored might of a 110-ship convoy. We saw German U-boats out in the ocean, but they were far enough away that they weren't going to take care of us. It was quite an experience, though, going all that way across the ocean.

Once we got to England, they took us, the Essex Scottish and the RHLI, the Royal Hamilton Light Infantry, which was part of our brigade, all of us officers had to go to where our bases were, which was Middleton-on-Sea, a beautiful town along the coast line. You were in the war zone because that's where the enemy was coming over at night. You could hear those German Fokkers in the air. Spitfires were everywhere. Those guys who flew those fighter planes, they were gutsy guys.

From Middleton-on-Sea they sent us to another officers school in Sandhurst, which was the big weapons training center in England. I became a weapons training officer. From the Essex Scottish unit, they moved four of us to brigade headquarters, No. 4 Brigade.

Brigade No. 4 headquarters was in Southern England. It was located there so that the Germans didn't know what the Allies were doing. Going there was like a step up towards being given a colonel's command. I was slotted to be invited. I'd been a commanding training officer, I'd been a weapons training officer with the Essex Scottish. At brigade, we had more meetings because we had communications links with the Polish tank brigade and the British infantry brigade and the free French. And the free French, some of them had actually dropped into France and then escaped back to England. Some of the things that happened after Dieppe, it's amazing how some of those intelligence people, British particularly, gained the information about the shoreline, where the German guns and munitions were located. They would actually be landing in there at night and getting out a couple of weeks later. They're the real unsung heroes because information is what they had to have to make an invasion work.

Getting prepared shortly before the June 6, 1944 D-Day invasion.

That was February 1944 and that's when we learned that D-Day was coming. They started to put people into place. You've been trained to go in. You'd been up to Scotland and done rope work up and down cliffs, been in water rescues where you've learned to keep your weapons dry at all times, because you've got to be able to fire them once you reach your objective.

We'd been waterproofed for about two or three weeks, so we knew something was coming soon. Every once in a while, we'd go out on midnight reconnaissance missions to see where the shells were coming from France. It was a little scary, but England had some great ideas. They used air balloons. When the Germans were lobbing shells in, the V1s and the V2s, they'd knock the balloons out. When you saw the red light on, you knew that everything was all right. But when you saw the red light go off, you knew the shell was coming down.

Getting ready for the assault when they took us to the Gulf of Thames and first we were in a big liberty ship out of London. We were only on there two days and they moved us to the English Channel. The Mulberry was already in the Channel, almost to the other shoreline. I'll never forget when we saw this Mulberry. They were artificial harbors constructed in British shipyards. Weighing several tons, these enormous concrete structures were towed across the Channel to serve as breakwaters and piers needed to aid the attack forces during the invasion. The tanks were on the Mulberry and there was a raft. As soon as the troops got in and there was an opening, they were going to get these tanks and the armor coming in and supplies, they had to get supplies in, food and ammo.

As we closed in on Normandy Beach, our objective, we had to get off the Liberty and get into an LCA, a landing craft assault vehicle. We had about 24 guys on board and a captain that controlled it. We were bobbing like a cork in the water and some of the guys were seasick right away. The poor guy who ran the thing said, "Don't worry, you get used to the smell." And it wasn't the motor he was talking about.

Guys were sick and everybody was scared. They didn't know what was going to happen. Then one guy with me, a sergeant, points up to the sky and says, "Captain Lynch, there's no place for the birds to fly." British planes were bumper-to-bumper going in to attack the coastline. Shells from the ships were lobbed into the shoreline and they were tearing up Normandy

Beach, where we were about to land. The Americans were landing at Omaha Beach, to our right.

In our unit, we had the British, we had the Canadians and of all things, the Polish tank brigade. Some of them had trained right here in Windsor.

You'd been briefed, we'd learned about what to expect and what not to expect. Once the beach was under control, they had claw machines to knock the mines out. And once they knocked them out, the landing craft would head towards that area. Troop personnel could get off. You went this way and you were up to your chest in water. You had to protect your gun and your pistol.

There had been a path cut because there were mines all along the shoreline. They had put a tag line so that if you saw yellow, you followed the yellow and you avoided the shell lines to get into shore. You hit the ground and you kept your fingers crossed that you were going to keep moving. I don't really talk about it, but it's a harrowing experience to know that human life is nothing when there's an invasion. And you feel sorry for the generals who have to make the decision that, "We want 1,500 troops to go in." Well, 1,500 tried getting through, but only 300 got to land. That's all.

All told, it's estimated that of the 100,000 Canadians who participated in Operation Overlord, as D-Day was properly known, 42,000 were wounded and 9,900 were killed.

I was sitting at the Windsor armories one night with a few of the old timers and this one sergeant said to me, "Do you talk about the war much?" I said, "No, not unless somebody asks me a question." Like most soldiers, we were scared. We'd volunteered, but we were still scared. Once you were ready to go in, you didn't know what to expect. I had a theory that if I could walk and talk, I could live. Where I got that theory from, I don't know. You don't reminisce much about the war years. Once in a while if someone asks, you talk. It's part of your history and you're lucky to be around to talk about it.

The impact of the war is still evident everywhere. At Grosse Isle Country Club, they trained some of the RAF pilots there during the war. There's 12 of them that never made it. They're buried in a cemetery on Grosse Isle, young kids from England, Scotland and Ireland who'd come over here to practice flying to get back over and be Spitfire pilots.

I've seen plenty of films about the war and D-Day. Some of the movies have been very truthful and accurate, while others have been more of a Hollywood style. I'll give you an example of Hollywood getting it wrong. Being in the infantry, say you're on this wall and you've got to go across to that wall to see where the enemy is located. You wouldn't dare run across an open gap, like the soldiers so often do in the movies, because you'd be an easy target. You'd take the long way around to get to the other side.

When it was finally time to come in, Germany blew it, I always felt, as a study of war history over the years. They could have knocked off that whole beach and we would have never got our supplies in to the troops. If they had knocked out the Mulberry, if they had knocked out the area where they had to get the tanks in, there would have been almost three feet of water before the Allies could get up on the beach. The Germans could have bombed that shoreline and could have wiped out that invasion within 24 hours, but the paratroopers went in behind the lines and nullified them getting to the coast line. And the intelligence for the guys in the tanks and the guys driving the Bren gun carriers, that really gave the Allies the edge. And then the ability to keep the supplies coming, once you're in there for three or four days, that was another huge factor.

The leaders really did a great job in the planning of the invasion. I give U.S General Dwight D. Eisenhower credit. He was in charge. He had to make a difficult decision and he did. The weather was changing, and time was of the essence. British Prime Minister Winston Churchill, what a stubborn man he was, but a brilliant guy for sure. I've read a couple of his books. He was a tough one.

I saw the cliffs at Omaha Beach and how those American Rangers were able to scale those cliffs is beyond me. And once they get to the top, they'd be dealing with machine-gun fire and pillboxes. Those Rangers were brave guys.

The American groups, their one desire, their fervent dream, was to get to Paris. We were OK with that because we knew the Germans were going to be all around there.

I regret that I haven't gone back to Normandy. Maybe I'll work it out yet. They treat you royally when you go back if you were part of the invasion force.

We got through D-Day in the afternoon and now we were in France. We were called the left of the line troop. Once you got in, you didn't know how far the enemy was retreating. They were retreating, but they were leaving behind land mines, so you couldn't drive any of the roads. If you goofed, goodbye.

It was a very stressful time, so you didn't eat very much. We had rations, but you didn't feel like eating. You'd have a chew on something. Survival, that was the name of the game.

We were going to Cherbourg and our first objective was Carpiquet Airfield. About the fourth day on shore, we were into this area and we knew the airport was just over there. The Allies wanted to control that because then they could bring in their helicopters, and gliders and get more troops into the area. But it was all mined, so the corps of engineers were in there blasting mines everywhere. Well, when we got there, it didn't look like a runway when we saw it because, boy; there were potholes everywhere.

Afterwards, we had to move left of that, going toward a place called Caen. Caen and then Falaise Gap, those were our objectives. Brigadier Sherwood Lett, who was in World War I, he was our top man at brigade headquarters, a little short guy, a real tough soldier. He should never have been up front with us, but he was too stubborn. He said, "Come on, Lynch, we're going." It was July 28, 1944, and we went down this hedgerow looking for a German machine-gun nest. We knew there were machine gun posts hidden, but we didn't know where they were. Well, we get down there and bump into these two kids, 13-year-old Panzer kids. They could have killed us, because when we approached, they took out their hand grenades, pulled the pin and held them in their hands. If they let go, they were gone, but we'd have been gone, too. They were scared, but they surrendered. We stripped them of their weapons and then we went about another 10 yards and these Moaning Minnies started coming over.

Moaning Minnies were shells that are about three inches in diameter and the Germans were lobbing them everywhere. One type was a solid shot, for armor piercing, another kind was high explosive and the other kind was smoke-filled. The noise they made sailing through the air gave them their name.

A Moaning Minnie hit me. The shell was three inches in diameter, but luckily, it was a solid shot that went right through my shoulder. I could feel the flesh, but I didn't know how badly I was hurt. We were commando trained, so I took the shell dressing and had the German kid grip my hand to control the nerves. Then Lett gets hit in the side of the head and he has to have the other kid bandage him up. We finally got back to a farmhouse area, almost a quarter of a mile away, where there was a doctor's forward post. Both Lett and myself had been hit pretty hard, but we didn't realize it.

They put me on a stretcher and Father Mike Dalton, who was our chaplain, he looks down at me, takes my dog tag and says, "Yep, it's you, Budd." They had me taped up like a mummy, so I said, "Does everything look all right?" So he says, "I'm here to administer you the last rites of the church." He's still alive, about 100 years old now and I talk to him every so often and say, "I'm still here."

The forward field medical unit, two young doctors whose names I never got, made up their mind to take the bone out, the scapula and take the arm off and gauze me up. I met one of them years later and he told me he'd never practiced medicine before he treated me. He'd gone into the army after graduating medical school and they'd sent him to the front-line medical units.

Then they put me in a stretcher and sent me to an American forward field hospital on the shoreline of France. I was there for about two days and then they flew me back to England to the No. 1 Canadian hospital, which was on Lord and Lady Astor's estate. The grounds were beautiful, and I'll tell you the nice thing about it - there were guys from the army, the navy and the air force and there were even some German officers who were prisoners in one of the wings and they took such great care of us it was unbelievable. Lady Astor, she was a teetotaler, and the doctors -- after we'd been there about a week prescribed Guinness stout for us. They said we could have a little Guinness stout, which all the guys thought was a great idea. But whenever Lady Astor would come out to make her visit, which was just about every other day, the orderly would have to hide the bottles of Guinness behind the blackout curtains until she left so she wouldn't find out.

One day, I decided I wanted to get some money from my account with the Bank of Montreal in London. The courier came along and I wrote a check for five quid. I don't know why, I wasn't going anywhere. I don't know what I wanted five quid for, but I did. Two days later the courier comes back and says, "Your signature is not recognizable." "That's right," I thought. "I've got to remember that." I'd been a right-hander all my life and now I was going to have to learn to do all of my tasks left-handed. So I went down to the Red Cross blackboard every morning to practice writing until I could get my name right. Eventually, I got my money, so there I am with five quid, but I'm still not going anywhere

I learned to write southpaw, and I'd send letters home to my mother from the hospital, and here's an amazing thing: she kept them and she kept the letters I had written before I lost my arm, and my writing turned out to be exactly the same as it was before. So the old story they say that right brain controls your left side and your left brain controls your right side, it looks like it's right.

For exercise, they made you go out and play croquet. I'd get out there with some of the legless guys in wheelchairs and some guys with one arm or one leg and we're all out there playing croquet. I said, "I won't be sticking with this sport." My mental thoughts were that I didn't know what I was going to do.

Eventually, an idea hit me. For some reason, I'm coming along pretty good, I'm getting up out of the hospital bed and moving around down the hallway, seeing some of the other guys, and I was stubborn and I decided, "If I can do this much, I've got to stay over here, rehabilitate myself and get a job in London."

Cam Ritchie was working for the Armed Forces radio then. He didn't go into France. One day I talked the doctors into getting me a chance to go to London to see if I could get a job producing shows. They gave me an orderly, put me on the subway and got me into London, and I saw Cam and Colonel Sampson with the Canadian Armed Forces radio. They were tied in with the Americans, too. They saw that I was interested and said, "Oh sure. You've got broadcasting experience and combat experience, and you want to rehabilitate yourself and help others." And I said, "Yeah, I do."

I came back to the hospital and got a 30-day permit to go and work with the guys. It was fascinating. Cam Ritchie and I shared an office with two other guys in the Langham Hotel, which was part of the BBC's superstructure. One of the adjoining offices was Glenn Miller's, the famous American bandleader.

The payoff was in my production work. I did a show at 4:45 in the morning called Combat Diary, where they took a report on all the theaters - the Italian theater and what was happening there, what was happening in Sicily. It was all correlated by the British Intelligence and then we, in turn, would voice it shortwave to forward field units so they'd know that everything was going fine down there, that Montgomery was having success there. We got cited by Eisenhower and Churchill for it.

Anyway, now it's December 1944, and I had produced shows with Bob Farnon, who used to be with the Happy Gang in Toronto, Glenn Miller and George Melachrino, a great English musician who was a regimental sergeant major as well, and I was about to become part of one of the great mysteries of the latter stages of World War II, the disappearance of Glenn Miller.

Miller's orchestra, formed in 1938, turned him into an American icon. They produced 70 top-10 records in a scant four years. The legendary American bandleader and his musicians enlisted to aid the war effort. He attained the rank of major and Glenn Miller's Army Air Force Band performed all over England, entertaining the Allied troops. It was Dec. 15, 1944, and he was slated to fly a Norsemen C-64 airplane to Paris to make final arrangements for a Christmas concert in the French capitol.

The day that Miller allegedly went to the airport to take off for Paris, my show was at 4:45 in the morning and I'd wrap it up by about 5:30, so I had breakfast in the BBC cafeteria with Miller's band. They'd gone to the airport and they'd brought them back. Nobody was getting off the ground because it was socked in with fog. As a result, everybody said, "What happened to Miller?"

Scotland Yard called early in the day. Cam and I were in the same office and they wanted to know how well we knew him. Well, we knew Miller as a great musician, a popular guy, but a loner. I said, "He just wanted to be in Paris before his band got there." It was one of those ego things. They said, "What do you think happened?" "He never got off the ground," I said. During the war, you didn't have a private plane. They were all military planes. And you couldn't get petrol. "How the hell could he get off the ground?" I said. If somebody was going to flip him over to Paris from Croyden, it was a very short flight, but there was nothing flying that day. "If he got into any plane, it's on the cliffs of Dover or somewhere in the English countryside," I told them.

The Scotland Yard guys were really nice, but they were thorough in their questioning. "Did you ever drink with him? Did you ever eat with him?" We didn't really know who he was. We did his show a couple of times with him there, but that was about it.

There are plenty of theories of what happened to Miller that day. Some feel the plane took off and later crashed in poor weather conditions. Others purport that it was brought down by friendly fire. To this day, no one knows the real answer for certain.

Tex Beneke was his No. 2 man, a brilliant guy. He used to tour this area quite a bit, and I went to see him once. He said, "You were the crazy guy in the kilt, weren't you?" He remembered what I wore.

Later on, I went up to Scotland and they had World War I doctors up there who realized that I was interested in getting an artificial right arm, a prosthesis. They worked with me over a period of about three weeks to design one. I had it so that on the artificial right hand I had been fitted with was equipped with a thumb catch, so I could put the script in there when I was emceeing a show. It was heavy and awkward to put on, but it served its purpose.

I wore it, except a couple of times when we'd go out in London during the blackouts with a couple of the guys I was living with. I'd take the arm off, so I'd have my sleeve tucked into my waistband. I'd had a couple of nips late at night in this one bar. We were taking the subway home and they'd say to me, "We're short today on knives, forks, spoons and ashtrays." They'd put all the utensils down my empty sleeve. I'd get on that subway going rattle, rattle, rattle. It's a good thing they didn't have metal detectors in those days, or I would have been caught for stealing.

The One-Armed Bandit

CHAPTER THREE

" *Assess a man for what he has . . .
not what he has not."*

- War Amps Motto

On Christmas Day, 1944, I got the call that they wanted me back in Montreal. They wanted military experienced personnel, an officer out of combat and a broadcaster with experience to head up the Armed Forces of the CBC International. That's how I got back from Europe and where I spent the rest of the war until 1945.

Coming back to North America, they put me on the Queen Mary, which was an American hospital ship. On board, there were amputees from the army, navy and air force, guys with legs off, patches over their eyes. We got an afternoon card game, cocktail and R&R session going on the ship.

There were five of them who had their arms off besides me. I'd sit and give lessons every afternoon on how to play cribbage, euchre and gin with one arm. It's simple, really. You take a hair brush and turn it upside down and put the cards in the bristles. One guy said, "What about bridge?" So I came up with an idea. I took a Kleenex box and sliced it lengthwise with a knife. There was just enough room in the slit for 13 cards.

We'd have these raging card games every day. One afternoon, I put my kilt on and I came strolling in and a couple of the guys said, "Here he comes again, the one-armed bandit." So that's where the phrase came from and I use it all of the time. The one-armed bandit - I've called myself that for years.

Those are the kinds of things I've tried to do to help others out. That's been a great thing for me, to be able to help out people. I taught people in my service days how to lace up their shoes, because I did it myself for about five or six years until, after a while, Velcro was available and it was a fast way to get dressed.

I was always willing to help anyone out who asked. Someone would say, "OK, give me a lesson today." And I'd say, "OK, we're going out to dinner." What I do when I go out to dinner and people get mad at me because of it, but I take the knife, fork and spoon and I put them in front of me, not on the left or right. I put them where I can reach it. Now there's room for the drink.

A lot of people get embarrassed when they go out because they think other people should cut their meat for them. Well, if it's too tough, send it back to the chef. But I taught them a way to cut the meat. There's a grain in meat. I designed a weapon and that's what they called it, too and I should have patented the damn thing. Instead, I told everybody what it was. When I was in Scotland, they fixed up my artificial arm. They were teaching me how to do things with my left hand, eating in particular. A fork and a spoon, that's what you need. Anyway, they took the fork and they filed the one prong down to where it was like a blade. And then they took the end of the fork and hammered it and cupped it so it looked like a spoon and then bent it. You could carry it with you every place you went. You had the one blade, the fork and the spoon. I had several of them made up and given to all the amputees I knew up there. Later on, I thought, "Oh geez, I should have got a patent on that."

Those are just some of the tricks of the trade that you pass on to other people. Like tying ties, for instance. Every place I went in the military, I had to tie my own ties. I had to figure out how to do it. You never look in a mirror when you're tying a tie. You do it all mentally.

The guys I used to get so mad at are the ones who would rely on their wives to do their shoes up, to tie their ties, to button their shirt. They'd get mad at me for saying it, but I was right.

When I got to Montreal, I went in for my medical and immediately, they took my artificial arm off. "You can't wear that, Budd," the doctor told me. "You have no idea what it's doing to your heart muscles." It weighed 40 pounds. And he said, "Within two years, you'll have a welt there that you'll never get rid of. You've got to get rid of it.'" Right in the examining room, he took it off of me. So now I knew that I was a wingee for sure. I thought, "How the hell am I going to start driving?" so I started thinking again.

It's simply the power of suggestion. You've got to go out and try something. I guess it's like everything else. When I came back from overseas, I had driven in the blackouts in England with one arm. You didn't do much driving over there, but we did have access to vehicles. And over there, most of your driving is on the other side of the road, so for a left-hander, it's perfect. But when I came back to Montreal, it was a whole new world.

I didn't apply in Montreal for a driver's license. I waited until I got to Hamilton, Ontario, on my way back to Windsor. I picked my wife Fran up and I said, "I think I'll wait to Windsor before I apply for my driver's license," so she drove the car most of the way to Windsor.

As soon as we got there, I went down to apply. They didn't want artificial limbs, but they had steering knobs on steering wheels. I'd seen them and I said, "No, I don't want a steering knob, for two reasons - It could injure your funny bone and then you'd be paralyzed, or it could catch in your sleeve." It's false security. On my license for the first three years it said I had to have a steering knob. So I had it on there, tucked underneath.

You learned to use your forearm to help you drive. You had to practice at it a little, but with time, you developed control. When I moved to the States, it was the same thing. I had to reapply for a driver's license. I'd done a show with the secretary of state's office and I told them the same thing. "I don't believe in that steering knob." They had all of these Hollywood gimmicks out there, but I said the same thing - it's false security. That thing could unscrew. I said, "If I have to have it . . ." "You have to have it," they said. Left-side turn signals and a steering knob, they were both mandatory.

When I first came back from overseas, the War Amps in Hamilton got a hold of my wife Fran and said, "We'll send some arm amputees over to see you and let you know what it's going to be like to put up with some of the things you'll have to go through for awhile." Later, I became very active in the Southwestern Ontario chapter of the War Amps, the Windsor branch. I emceed a lot of shows for them and had some great golf tournaments. Their credo, "Assess someone for what they have, not for what they have not," I think that's a credo that's important in life.

At first, I wondered what I'd do for hobbies. I kept kidding myself, "I know, I'll be a fisherman," because I used to fish before. I also played golf before. When I first came to Windsor, I'd go down to Beach Grove and play.

After the war, in 1946, one day I went back to Beach Grove. Bill Dennis was the pro. He said, "You're interested in golf, are you?" I said, "Yeah, but I couldn't break 100 with two arms." He said, "OK, we'll practice." I'd go down there maybe three days a week and practice two or three holes. Then he took me down to Lakewood, the golf course near Beach Grove, about a month later and I had a 99 the first time I played with one wing. "OK," Bill said. "I guess you've got the bug now." I'll tell you, when I get out there and play, I don't get any sympathy from the other guys when I start beating them, but it's a lot of fun.

Returning to Windsor, I was back again working with CKLW and doing the play-by-play of the Windsor Spitfires for two years. Jack Dulmage of The Windsor Star, who's in the writer's section of the Hockey Hall of Fame, and I had worked together at Spitfires games and we had some great times. Jack smoked a pipe, and I've smoked a cigar all my life. On the team bus, Jimmy Skinner, the Spitfires coach, would put us in the back of the bus and general manager Lloyd Pollock would come back and sit with us so that he could have a cigar.

The Ontario Hockey Association Junior A Series, as it was known back then, was tremendously competitive. All of the teams in those days were sponsored by National Hockey League clubs, who supplied the teams with talent from all over the country, prospects for the pros. I broadcasted some great games in Barrie, Guelph, Galt and at Maple Leaf Gardens, where the Toronto Marlboros and St. Michael's Majors played.

Some of the rinks where the games were played weren't exactly up to snuff, though. Windsor Arena was like a barn that should have been condemned. Hamilton's Barton Street Arena was like a barn that should have been condemned. In fact, almost every building in the league should have been condemned. In Hamilton, they had rafters, beams supporting the seats that you'd even see when you'd go into the dressing rooms.

The broadcasting locations also left a lot to be desired. Not exactly first-rate facilities. I remember we did a game in Barrie, Ontario, which was a Boston-sponsored club and our broadcasting location was a crossbeam over the ice. We sat on it and were looking down on the ice. Dulmage was off to one side and there were fans sitting up there with us. There's this skirmish by the Spitfires bench. I remember saying, "I think there's two gendarmes in this whole place and one of them is over by (Windsor coach) Jimmy Skinner, and he's about to discover that Skinner is a lefthander." This guy grabs the mic from me and says, "You can't say that." I grabbed the mic back and continued. ". . . As I was saying, there's a skirmish by the visitor's bench and Jimmy Skinner is a lefthander and he'll deck somebody if they get too close." The same guy grabs the mic again and says, "I'm the mayor of Barrie." So I got the mic back and I said, "I guess the mayor of Barrie wants to tell me that there's more than two gendarmes here tonight." Dulmage just started laughing. "They're going to put you in jail, weren't they?" he said. "Yes, I think they were going to put me in jail," I replied. Those are the sorts of things that would happen in the course of covering a sport during that time.

I'll give the Butcher family, who owned the Windsor Arena, a lot of credit, though. They spent a lot of money trying to fix the place up for junior hockey and other entertainment purposes.

Entertainment purposes for which I wasn't too shy to make suggestions.

I had a brain wave one time. I told my boss at CKLW, Ted Campeau, "I think we should bring some entertainment in here." He said, "that's a good thought." So I got a hold of Bill and Les Butcher, the owners of the rink and said, "I'm going to bring the Happy Gang down here from Toronto." Well, the Happy Gang was the bible for people who listened to radio out of Toronto. They were a CBC musical variety show that aired regularly at lunchtime between 1937-59 and some of the people who were part of the Happy Gang included Bert Pearl, Bob Farnon, Blaine Mathe, Eddie Allen, Herb May and Bobby Gimby.

We brought them down and drew 9,000 people to the show the first night. That wet the whistle, so I decided to bring in more acts. I brought in Lou Baron, the big band leader and we had about another 9,000 people in for that show. We made it no drinking in the place, so it could also be for the kids. The next move I made came after I found out that a lot of the name bands were playing Ottawa, Toronto, London, then going to Chicago. So I figured between London and Chicago, they could stop in Windsor.

I got a hold of Louis (Satchmo) Armstrong's agent and I explained to him on the phone that, "I know you're playing London on Wednesday night. Why don't you come and play the Arena in Windsor on Saturday night?" The guy said, "Well, I'll send my wife down." She did all of their booking. But he wanted to know, "Where are you going to accommodate us?" In those days, a lot of hotels wouldn't take black customers. So I got a hold of the Prince Edward Hotel in downtown Windsor and they took over the whole second floor. Louis had three or four white musicians, but most of them were African-Americans. He was such an entertainer. He played a half hour extra because the crowd was so warm to him. Afterwards, he said, "You've got a good idea here. Book more bands." So what did I do? I came over and took a job in the States.

As my first wife Fran and our five daughters look on. I officially become a U.S. Citizen.
Notice I had to raise my left hand to be sworn in by Judge Frank Picard in Dearborn.
Mich.

Getting a little elevation with the help of world champion wrestler Whipper Billy Watson
following a 1948 interview at the CKLW studio.

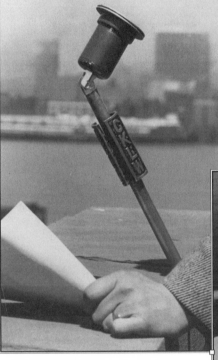

(above) I went back to work at CKLW in Windsor after returning to my hometown following World War II. (right) In my booth at Olympia Stadium. I began my play-by-play career with the Wings in 1949.

I was invited back to Windsor to emcee the opening of the Elmwood Casino. I had met Al Siegel, who owned the Elmwood, before. That was a great place. They had three different restaurants and all kinds of entertainment in the place. The opening night, you couldn't get in the place. At first, the Canadians weren't sure if they liked the idea of the place, but after a while, they really warmed to it. You had a Cantonese Restaurant, an American restaurant and a Canadian restaurant. There was ample room to sit in those restaurants and listen to who was playing in the big room. If you wanted to see them in the big room, you paid extra money and sat at tables where you could see the entertainment. Some of the acts who appeared there over the years included Sammy Davis Jr., Sonny and Cher, Jimmy Durante, Sophie Tucker, The McGuire Sisters, Lena Horne, Tom Jones and Peggy Lee, along with many others.

Years later, I got a call from a very good friend of mine telling me that it had become an Alcoholics recovery center, the Brentwood Recovery Home for Alcoholics.

I did a crazy thing at the Windsor Armories one time. I was president of the junior chamber of commerce, and I got an idea to hold a trade show there. I got a hold of WWJ-TV to bring their equipment over to shoot. We had subsidiary companies such as Ford and Chrysler which had booths there. It was a made in Canada show, that was the idea. When the show was over, the TV crew took a while to pack up and when they cleared customs, they got a notation. Washington had called. It didn't come from Ottawa because my boss had got clearance from them. They were beaming a picture across an international border without permission from the government. My boss had to go to Ottawa and read a statement and a Washington lawyer had to take care of it. Wire photos had been sanctioned to cross the border back then, but television hadn't. It was one of things you didn't think about. It was a scary moment for me.

Another crazy event that happened to me while I was working at CKLW involved Orville Hubbard, who was the mayor of Dearborn. He'd been at a mayor's convention in Calgary and on the way back, he found out he was going to be served with a million-dollar lawsuit if he set foot on American soil. So he stopped in Windsor and took over the second floor of the Prince Edward Hotel and called it the Dearborn annex. He was there for about 10 days.

Since I worked for the Mutual Network, CKLW sent me down there to interview him every Monday, Wednesday and Friday. He got a great deal of publicity. He was all over the country, talking about running the office on Canadian soil while he was still mayor of Dearborn.

Years later, when we finally moved to the States and settled in Dearborn, we'd been there maybe two weeks and gotten to know our neighbors and I said, "How do you get passes to Camp Dearborn?" They said, "Just get in touch with city hall and they'll send them to you, or you can go and pick them up."

So I called on a Saturday morning and said, "I'm new in the area and I was wondering how I could get credentials for my car. I've got some relatives coming and I want to take them to see Camp Dearborn." The fellow on the phone said, "Say that again." So I said, "I'm new over here, how do I apply to get credentials?" Then the fellow said, "Is that you, Budd?" It was Orville, answering the phone on Saturday morning. We talked for about 20-25 minutes. He says that it's fantastic that I'm in the States, he was told I was coming over and he said, "I want to put you on the recreation committee." I said, "I can't. I'm a Canadian; I'm not an American. You can't put me on anything." Well, don't you know it, a little while later, two squad cars pull up in front of the house. They give my wife and the kids stickers, vouchers, credentials for the boat rides out there. My neighbors didn't talk to us for three weeks. Those Canadians come over here and there's two squad cars at their door the first Saturday morning. Then they found out about how I'd known Orville from my Windsor days and everything was OK.

Orville served as mayor of Dearborn from January 1, 1942, to January 1, 1973, and there's a statue of him outside the Dearborn City Hall on Michigan Ave. He was a character, but he had some really great ideas. He took over a piece of property and with Dearborn money, he built Camp Dearborn, which was just a beautiful set-up. They had two lakes, a camping site and a summer camp for boys and girls. Three of my kids went there. They taught crafts, they went fishing and they had those paddle boats. It was a great idea and it was part of Dearborn, out near Hudson, Michigan. Eventually, they built a golf course. It got to be very, very popular.

He opened up a senior citizens place in Florida, a high-rise for people from Dearborn. It could accommodate maybe 40 couples. You could go down there if you were from Dearborn and for about $200, you got 10 days vacation.

One of the distinct advantages I found working with CKLW was that with the station being part of the Mutual Radio Network, it gave me opportunities to branch out and cover some very significant events.

CKLW was one of the original stations in the Mutual network. CKLW had a Detroit studio as well as a Windsor studio. Other stations included WOR in New York and WGN in Chicago. Mutual was a growing network and Van Patrick, who'd become a famous Detroit sportscaster, was working for them, too. He didn't know how far they were going to expand, but they were into news and they were into sports. I think having had that experience in Windsor became a big plus for me. When I worked at CKLW, I did sports in the morning. Then we'd go to the Detroit studio in the Guardian Building and we'd tape shows for the Mutual network people around the country, and I'd do the voice over. It gave you an indication that the broadcasting field was getting bigger and bigger and that TV was developing into a network. It also scared you at times.

Mel Allen, the legendary New York Yankees broadcaster, was a great guy. I worked with him on the Mutual network on a Notre Dame football game one time in South Bend. What a thrill. I'd been on the campus before, because a few of my buddies from Hamilton had gone to Notre Dame. But now we're in the stadium, up in the broadcast booth for the football game. We had the last booth and the old press box in South Bend, they had these slats, support beams in the roof. Mel was 6-foot-2 and I'm 6'1", so we had to keep ducking to get to our booth. We get down there, we're on the air and Mel says, "What do you think of our location? We've got a beautiful view of the football field." I said, "I think the Hunchback served his apprenticeship trying to get here." Jokingly, you know. Well, Mel got about 150 letters from alumni all over the country who thought he'd said it. I learned a lesson that day. You don't criticize anybody at Notre Dame.

Working for the Mutual network, I was asked to do Detroit Lions games, Michigan and Michigan State football. I had a thrill with Mel Allen doing a game at East Lansing. They were going to bring colored television in. We had to go there on the Friday because they were going to do a dry run. The cameras for the color TV, they were 4 ½ to 5-feet long. They wanted to do a test to see how it worked. It was overcast, it was grey and everything worked perfectly. They put wrappers on the cameras overnight. Come Saturday, it rained and by the third quarter, everything was back to black-and-white. The colors, the blues, the reds, all faded. The camera lens could only take so much light. In the early days of television, the original show was a four poster bed. They had two cameras and it was all the same scene, so they didn't have to worry about following the action. It was nothing like trying to cover sports.

Harry Wismer was another guy I worked with on college football and Detroit Lions games. His brother owned a radio station up in Port Huron. Harry was an outspoken character. We're doing this one game at Ann Arbor, and for the first 15 minutes, he spent the whole time leaning out of the booth and he started naming off names, you know, name-dropping. "There's so-and-so, the vice-president of Chrysler and with him is the president of Chrysler . . ." He named about five guys. Well, somebody in the stands had a radio and came up to see him at halftime. "Harry, you blew it again," the guy said. "Three of the guys you named are in Germany right now." You've got to be careful when you're doing a live broadcast.

I figured I'd hold on to the hockey as long as I could and do these other things. It worked out well, but I don't think you could do it today. They want you to be under the control of sponsors, stations, or advertisers. And once that happens, everything changes.

I had relatives stateside and I'd been over there. One day, I was standing by the water, looking across the river at Detroit and a couple of young people said to me, "Are you dreaming about going over there?" And I said, "No, I've been over there. That's why I'm on this side." Little did I know I'd soon come to eat those words.

Mutual wanted me to go to Chicago in 1948. I was raising kids and I said, "No, I don't want to go that far away." About six months later, they wanted me to go to Detroit, which was close to home.

That old phrase about being in the right place at that right time comes to mind.

Winging It In A New Medium

CHAPTER FOUR

❝ *Let's give the one-armed guy a try."*
- Jack Adams

Ty Tyson from the Detroit News, he was the sports director at WWJ and they were getting into television in the late 1940s. He wanted me to produce shows because I had done some producing when I was overseas. Paul Williams insisted I come over and so did Van Patrick, two other prominent Detroit sportscasters.

I worked for the Mutual network because CKLW was part of Mutual in those days. Van and I knew each other from way back. I went over to Detroit from Windsor in the summer of 1949. My wife Fran and I had three little girls and we settled in Dearborn. It was one of those rare opportunities. The training camp was coming up for the Red Wings, so the News sent me up to the training camp. That's where I met Bruce Martyn for the first time. He was working at the radio station up there and his wife was the secretary for the station.

Paul Williams had been doing hockey, but Stroh's, the sponsor of the games, didn't care for his work. Paul didn't know hockey. He was a football guy.

I owe an awful lot to Jack Adams, the general manager of the Red Wings at the time, who'd run the club since 1927. He's the one who gave me the chance, coming into the States to work on the broadcasts on a temporary basis. He said, "give the one-armed guy a try. He's played the game and he's broadcasted Windsor Spitfires' games." He knew I'd been around hockey.

I never had a contract in my life. I was a freelancer. I worked on a handshake. When I came to WWJ, I found out that I could make more money as a freelance announcer. I took a chance, but that's how I wound-up doing Michigan and Michigan State football games. Being available at the right time and not having a station or sponsor conflict, I was very fortunate in all those years that I could do hockey.

Al Nagler and I worked that first year. We did about five or six television games, too, but the radio coverage with Al was very interesting. Al was a fly boy in the American service and he admitted to me at different times that he hated flying and he hated heights. I said, "I thought you were a fly boy?" But he admitted, "I close my eyes when I fly." In Montreal for this first game, we're sitting on this ledge, looking down and if the play was going right to left, he never saw the left winger because he was too frightened to lean out and have a look. He had to wait until the play moved to the middle of the ice. Going the other way, he never saw the right winger. He only ever saw two forwards. He admitted he was scared.

Televised sports was a whole new world to all of us. When you're broadcasting radio at an early stage, you knew that you were selling the sport. Hall of Famer Ernie Harwell from the Detroit Tigers and I often talked about the same thing. In the radio days of broadcasting, you were informing the listener, no matter where they were - at home, in their car, on a boat. You were painting a picture, letting the person visualize what was going on. You mention the size of the puck, how high a player raised his stick on the back-swing of a shot, little things like that. You were adding things all of the time, making people feel like they were there. You did an awful lot of talking on radio in those days. But that's the way you get the listener advised. You didn't do too many commercials, either, and if you had a color man, the color man just added to what you had said or picked out something else to talk about. As the years went on, working with Al, who also did play-by-play like I did, we developed a companionship. We had a happy relationship. The same thing when Bruce and I got into it together. He had a happy capacity for never talking about the same thing as me. Radio is about always adding more.

When you get into TV, I remember the first games we broadcasted at the Olympia, we had two cameras. You added words to the pictures. But with two cameras, there's not too much to add. Fred Huber, the Wings' publicity director who did the color with me for one year, he talked an awful lot, but unless the director had the picture of what you were talking about - say there's a struggle behind the net and the camera is on it, you talk about it. That's TV. Otherwise, the camera could be panning the crowd. You had to develop a different style and approach to the sport. You're not doing the flow of the game like you did on radio.

The first game we did at the Olympia, I looked around at the two camera guys and there was one that I knew. I said, "Davey, what are you doing here?" And he said, "I've got seniority for overtime." I asked, "Do you know anything about hockey?" And he said, "I've never seen a hockey game." The poor director was just going nuts. I could hear him saying on the headset, "Dave, stay on the Grand River end of the building. Take it from the blueline to the goal and don't move off of that area. Don't go up an down the ice like you're trying to do."

I remember during the intermission of that first game, we had to turn to the side to one camera to talk and Fred, he talked non-stop for 18 minutes. A doctor friend of mine from Windsor who I knew from the war years sent a wire to the team and it said, "It's a shame that your knowledgeable P.R. director talks so much and that poor one-armed man was left to hold his microphone for the entire intermission."

On the train coming back from Montreal the next week, Jack Adams said, "Meet me in my suite in five minutes. I've got Fred coming in." We got in there and Jack read the wire aloud. Fred didn't say a word. Then he turned to me and said, "Didn't you say anything the whole time we were on?" And I said, "I didn't have a chance." Fred laughed about it.

When you were calling a game, you couldn't be a homer; you had to describe exactly what was going on. Unfortunately, as the years have gone on, talking to veteran broadcasters about this, on TV, there's too much talking today, too many camera angles and statistics. In watching TV in every sport, the stats, they drive me nuts. Even in golf, there's too much talking. Three guys in the booth, somebody on the course. I don't know whether we've overdone it, but I don't know how we're going to curb it, either. As an individual watching a sport, you want to watch it. That's the one good thing about boxing. You can't do much about it other than to focus on the one thing, the two fighters in the ring. Hockey and baseball and football, they've got reams and reams of stats and figures. I think Mickey Redmond and Ken Daniels, Detroit's current TV broadcasters, they've admitted it, too, that they get carried away with where the player came from, how he was traded. After a while, you don't hear what they've said because there's just too much talking.

I don't know if there's a happy way to do it or not, but as a broadcaster in the early days of broadcasting, I harken back to one the original broadcasters with the Montreal Canadiens when I started, Doug Smith. Doug and I got to be very good friends. We always used to say, by the time you describe what you're seeing when a goal is scored, you've got to follow up right away and describe how it was scored. Who lost the puck, factors such as that. In radio coverage, you concentrate more and you are the eyes of the listener. But I must say, I enjoyed every minute of it while performing both jobs.

The games back then were on Channel 7 and were sponsored by Strohs. But two of the games that first season had to be on Channel 9 in Windsor because of schedule conflicts. Well, you couldn't have beer advertising on Canadian television in those days. Since Strohs couldn't have beer advertising on Channel 9, they found a compromise and advertised Strohs Ice Cream.

Stroh Brewery, I'll give them credit, they did the same thing all the years they were our sponsor. Jack Adams was the one who talked them into it, but they'd send Jack, Fred Huber, Alex Delvecchio, Ted Lindsay, trainer Lefty Wilson and myself - there'd be about five of us barnstorming through the state of Michigan and sometimes Ontario. We'd go to Lansing for a luncheon, then maybe some golf or some fishing. Then at night, we'd go to another service club for a dinner. They'd show the old black-and-white Stanley Cup films. And Adams started to preach all the way up north, in all of these different cities, telling everybody, "Get your service clubs to put up a rink. You need a rink up here." And he preached the gospel of having a rink in every area so that kids could skate, so that they could play hockey, get out on the ice and have some fun and that's the way many of the rinks in Michigan were started.

Our coverage was limited because not that many people had television sets, and at first, our signal only went as far as Lansing. Eventually it went a little further north. By 1953, the signal was going even further because they had come up with ways of relaying the signal.

In the early days, Paul Williams and I had an assignment every other Saturday. We had to go to St. John Berchmans gymnasium on Detroit's eastside, where they had wrestling matches. We had to go there at six o'clock to do a wrestling show from 6:30-7:30 p.m. The reason for it was that there were only about 400 television sets in all of Detroit at that time and half of them were owned by people who worked at The Detroit News, which also owned WWJ-TV. They wanted a wrestling show at the dinner hour. The wrestling was one hour long and we found innovative ways to add spice to the broadcast, to try to give the fans at home a sense that they were part of the action. Paul Williams would take a bag of peanuts and when one wrestler had another wrestler caught in a hold, Paul would be crunching the peanuts for sound effects.

With two minutes to go, the fight had to end, so Paul and I would have to slap on the canvas so that the guys would know it was time for one of them to get the pin. The same guys that wrestled in the exhibition from 6:30-7:30, they showered and ate, then went on again and wrestled for the fans who'd come to the gym to see it.

The wrestling was in demand. Boy the crowds they used to get for the wrestling and boxing shows at the Olympia was unbelievable. Former middleweight boxing champion Jake LaMotta was a very popular performer with the fans. But the wrestlers, they sure knew how to put on a show. Entertainment, that's what the building was to be used for. Even the Beatles came over from Britain and played there.

When you heard the old players reminisce, they often talk about the type of hockey they played in those days. They didn't use much equipment. They had very small shin guards and if a player got hurt, he'd never admit it, just put more tape on his wound. Some players would be out there with tape over their stockings. Protection from equipment was minimal in those days.

I think the original interpretation of what hockey was is that it was 60 minutes of sustained action. You didn't take many commercial breaks and there were very few stoppages of play. Sure, it's three periods, but for each of those 20-minute periods, there was something happening all the time. The crowd reacted because they were part of the game. There was chicken wire around most of the buildings at the time, so fans felt closer to the action. They could hear the players swearing.

I think a lot of women gained respect for hockey because they could go down by the dressing room and see what the guy looked like. For instance, Red Kelly with the red hair. When the game got going, if anybody hit Red, you'd hear some woman yell, "Don't you hit him." Those are the things that created the impact of understanding the sport. It's still a simple sport. Get the puck, get down the ice, shoot, if you don't score, get back and check.

I got to know and meet so many great people who'd been associated with hockey since the early days. You only had 120 players in the league. I'd go to the dressing room after the skate during the morning and I'd ask the trainer and I'd ask the players individually how they wanted their name pronounced. Today, the league gives you a list a phonetic spelling list of all the players. But in those days, some of the players had their own ideas. Real Chevrefils played for Boston and also later played for Detroit. Real told me one time before a broadcast in Boston, "Change my name today." I said, "To what?" "Chev-Ri-Feel, not Chev-re-fill," he said. "Why?" I asked. "There's people here who think I'm this kid from Moncton, New Brunswick and I can't get them any tickets," he explained

It was a tough job to sell the sport in New York, Chicago, Detroit, Boston, Montreal and Toronto. A lot of guys never got credit for keeping it going. There was competition in those days from many other events, but hockey always had a little bit of an inroad, a little bit of a following. You've got to give credit to radio first because radio sold the sport. Then television came in and dressed it up. But then they started experimenting in television. Why they wanted to color the boards or put a magnetic puck flying through the air, I'll never know or understand. Just go back to the basics, the speed and pace of this game is its greatest selling point.

I think of the Original Six teams and how many class players and class people there were involved with each of the clubs. The Patrick family, Muzz and Lynn and the old man from Vancouver, Lester, I met and got to know all of hockey's Royal Family, as they were referred to in that era. But you see, we played all of them seven times in each city. It was family, but it was competitive.

Every team, when you saw them enough, you respected their talent and their ability. Having met Toe Blake in my Hamilton days and later on, seeing his career, what a mastermind of hockey he was for the Montreal organization, coaching them to eight Stanley Cups. The Rocket, the Canadiens great star Maurice Richard, was just a rare individual. I never had any trouble talking to him, but a lot of the visiting writers used to say, "Don't go near him, he doesn't want to talk to anybody." Well, Maurice wanted to be talked to in French most of the time. That was the key to getting along with him.

It would be fun to watch Boston's Milt Schmidt take on Sid Abel for faceoffs, or Bill Gadsby take on Chicago's Stan Mikita in battles for the puck and for position on the ice. Faceoffs were the key thing. Puck possession was the key thing, but it's almost like a lost talent today. A lot of guys, they work at it. Stevie Yzerman was someone among today's players who was very good at it.

Naturally, playing each of the other five teams 14 times during a 70-game regular season led to some bad blood developing between players on some teams. There was a lot of stick swinging and when Toronto's Bill Ezinicki and Ted Lindsay went at it, boy it was a real duel. Those two were after each other every game, every shift and I'll tell you one thing, it was vicious. Ironically enough, Bill Ezinicki became a golf pro down in the Boston area and qualified for the U.S. Open one year when it was played at Oakland Hills. Ted Lindsay lived at that time just past the 15th green at Oakland Hills in a high rise, a nice home. So when Bill came in to play in the tournament, Ted went out and caddied for him. That was kind of a cute gesture.

That's what it was like in the NHL of that time. There was a deep-seeded fraternity among the players. Most of your athletes those days had the happy reality that if you lost your temper, if your lost your composure, you may get licked. But don't try to retaliate. And some of the players who tried to do that, their careers were very short.

There was also a bond among the journalists of the day who followed

The most powerful unit in Red Wings history - Ted Lindsay, Gordie Howe and Sid Abel - The Production Line.

the Red Wings. We traveled on the same train as the players during road trips. The photographers from the Detroit papers, Roy Bash and Scott Kilpatrick, even they traveled with us. The beat writers - Marshall Dan was the writer from the Free Press, Lew Walter from the Times, John Walter from the News and every so often, Jack Dulmage of the Windsor Star - they'd be along for the ride. You really developed a closeness in that sort of compartmentalized environment.

The players of the era were tough. You'd play over injuries because you didn't want to get sent to the minors. No way. But nobody knew, between the trainer and the coach, about injuries. Red Kelly played once with a broken hand. The officials in those days were a different breed of cat, too. There was much more communication between them and the players, because they all knew each other.

Today's athletes are entirely the opposite. There's big money to be made and the big egos that go along with that. The hockey people of that day, they came from humble beginnings and played a professional sport in six great cities. The season was over in April, the Stanley Cup was won in April and then they had to go back to their summer jobs. The western Canadian players returned to their farms and a lot of the other guys got jobs with breweries. I think players more appreciated the money they made. Certainly, winning a Stanley Cup was a thrill, but in those days, there was very little remuneration that came along with it.

Still, to win Lord Stanley's mug was the dream of every player and wouldn't you know it, the Wings would do exactly that during my first year on the job.

I've always believed that in life, a lot of it was being in the right place and the right time, and that's exactly what happened to me when I became the Red Wings broadcaster. I had such a good run. The four years of Stanley Cup wins between 1950-55, the two Game 7 Stanley Cup overtime final games, with Pete Babando and Tony Leswick scoring the goals. There's only been two Stanley Cup finals in NHL history decided on Game 7 overtime markers and I was fortunate enough to call both of them.

And like they say, you never forget that first one. Or that first season, for that matter.

The Wings rolled through the 1949-50 regular season accumulating a record 88 points, while Lindsay, Abel and Gordie Howe, the Production Line, finished 1-2-3 in NHL scoring, the only time three members of a Stanley Cup championship squad have ever done so. In the playoffs, they displayed their true character, rallying from 3-2 series deficits to defeat Toronto in the semifinals and the New York Rangers in the Cup final series, both of the series' decided by Game 7 overtime goals.

That first playoff year, the Wings are playing the New York Rangers in the final and the Rangers can't play their home games at Madison Square Garden because the circus is there, so they had to play in Toronto. Well, Toronto owner Connie Smythe was determined to make things as difficult for the Wings as he could. Smythe cut the price of tickets in half. He wanted to get as many people as he could in the building cheering for the Rangers, because he hated Detroit.

It was a good series, close all the way. Any overtime, boy the adrenaline flows for the players, for the fans, for the broadcasters and even some of the writers. You visualize so many things happening and you're mesmerized. You're still concentrating, seeing what players the coach is going to send out next, wondering if there's a fresh player on the bench that no one has thought about. Once you get past that first overtime anything can happen.

I recall the broadcast of that seventh game vividly. Pete Babando was the goal-scoring hero and it was tallied at 8:21 of the second overtime. He might have been the last guy you'd expect to get the goal. He was a non-noticeable player on the ice. When a line came on, you wouldn't know if Babando was out there or not. But he was a scooter.

The tension was building up because the Rangers had two or three great scoring opportunities early in the overtime and late in the third period, too. That's when you realized that it was a goalkeeper's paradise. Any overtime game, it's usually a fluke, or a break one way or the other, whether you make the break or you capitalize on somebody else's mistake. With the pace of hockey, even in those days, I think the mediocre hockey players and I include Babando in that category, they had one desire in life - to fire the puck at the net. It might go in. A lot of other players would stickhandle, gamble, try to go around defensemen, look to put the puck between his legs and go pick it up, but by the time you do that, you've usually lost control of the puck.

Talking to Hall of Fame pitcher Hal Newhouser the day of his last game as a Detroit Tiger in 1953.

Interviewing Champagne Tony Lema after his win in the first Buick Open in 1968. Lema was tragically killed in a plane crash the next day.

Babando certainly wasn't that kind of dipsy-doodle player. George Gee won the face-off back to Babando and Babando let his shot go from about 30 feet out, beat Rangers goalie Charlie Rayner about knee high on the stick side and the roof of the building seemed to come off.

Both teams were ready to celebrate. The Rangers had the Leland Hotel booked for their party, and the Red Wings had the Book-Cadillac Hotel booked for their party. Everyone was at the party now because the Red Wings had the Stanley Cup back and it wasn't Toronto or Montreal they had beaten—it was an American team. And that was an exciting year, my first year, too. And in retrospect, you'd hear the writers talk about it. I remember New York writer Stan Fischler said to me, "Your first year in hockey, they win the Stanley Cup against a Ranger team. Wouldn't it have been better if it had been against a Montreal team?" I said, "Any team." It didn't matter. The rivalry was always there in the international aspect of it.

Four years later, I called the other Game 7 OT Cup-winner, when the Wings edged the Montreal Canadiens for their third Cup in five seasons. That one stands out in my mind as well. We're in the last minute of play in regulation time, it's tied and I remember saying, "You can almost see a lucky shot going in to win this." And then we go to overtime and sure enough, a lucky shot goes in off a glove.

I can still almost visualize the shot in my mind. I can see Tony Leswick's drive going off the glove of Montreal defenseman Doug Harvey and dipping past Gerry McNeil in the Montreal goal. My first phrase was, "He has scored." I hadn't even used Leswick's name yet. Then while I was recapping, I realized what had happened, that I hadn't told anyone who scored the goal, so immediately I said it was Leswick. That was a hard-fought series and bitter, too, so bitter that the Canadiens wouldn't even shake hands afterwards.

It just shows you that anyone can be a hero. Of all the people to decide such dramatic Stanley Cup games, you never would have selected Babando or Leswick. But that's merely another element in what makes hockey the fabulous game that it is and gives you an example of the type of stuff that hockey players are made from.

Some of the things that are great credits to the boys who have played hockey as pros are their attitude and their fortitude. They've gone through the high school level, the college level and the minor-league level. They stuck with a sport they loved and the parents put up with the cost of travel and most of them are the same today, unlike other pro athletes.

These kids are willing to go out and visit with other kids at local rinks and give something back. It's a great tribute to those who play hockey. You don't find that in any other sport. Hockey players are always available, and I think they're the easiest athletes to interview, too.

That's A Fact, Jack

CHAPTER FIVE

" *Jack Adams, he was ahead of his time."*
                              - Budd Lynch

If there's one man in the Detroit Red Wings organization I owe a debt of gratitude to, it's Jack Adams. He opened the door for me, gave me the chance to become part of the club's broadcasting team in 1949.

Adams was the one who suggested to the Stroh Brewery company that they should, "Give the one-armed guy a chance." Paul Williams was the football guy at WWJ, and they didn't like his coverage of the sport. They were looking for a different voice.

I guess you could say I was one of many people in the game who was discovered by Jack Adams. When you think back to the era of longevity in professional sport, Connie Mack, who managed the Philadelphia Athletics from 1901-50, was the perfect example of how long can you stay in one place. The Connie Smythes, the Frank Selkes, the Jack Adams, the builders of our Canadian game of hockey, I've always felt that they never got enough recognition for all the things they did to get the thing going.

Adams came to Detroit in the spring of 1927, shortly after he'd finished his playing career, winning a Stanley Cup with the Ottawa Senators during the 1926-27 season. He'd also won a title with the Toronto Arenas in 1917-18, his rookie NHL season. He was a no-nonsense type of player, who could play the game in any manner required. Playing for the Vancouver Millionaires of the Pacific Coast Hockey Association in the 1920s, he was a two-time league all-star. Adams led the PCHA in scoring in 1921-22 and in penalty minutes during the 1920-21 campaign. As a player, he skated in three Stanley Cup finals.

He brought that same sort of determined attitude to his work behind the bench and early on, it was proving to be a difficult task for Adams. Known as the Cougars when he took over as coach-GM for the 1927-28 season, Detroit wasn't a powerful franchise and lacked the financial backing required to become a contender.

They tried everything to turn around their fortunes, even picking a new nickname - the Falcons - from a newspaper contest, but it wasn't until 1932, when shipping magnate James Norris purchased the club and changed the team nickname to the Red Wings, that Adams was finally able to combine his unique hockey mind with the resources necessary to build a winning program.

He wanted everybody who wore the Red Wings' uniform to represent the city of Detroit, the state of Michigan and parts of Ontario with pride. Most athletes in those days did. Whether they came from Western Canada or Quebec, he wanted them to feel that they were representing more than just the Red Wing hockey team. They were representing the kids who admired the men wearing those Red Wings' jerseys.

Jack was criticized at times for his hard-line stance on many issues, but sometimes, they didn't understand. Jack didn't drink. His father was an alcoholic and he admitted that. Jack had his own beliefs. When you put on that jersey, you were representing the Red Wings, the state of Michigan and parts of Ontario. He preached this to the players who wore the Red Wings jersey. Don't disgrace it. Don't get into trouble and whatever you do, don't drink too much.

Jack Adams, he was ahead of his time. He insisted on going up to Sault Ste. Marie for training camp. They had a beautiful, cold barn there, the Pullar Arena. There was hockey on both sides of the border there - in Sault Ste. Marie, Ontario, and Sault Ste. Marie, Michigan. It worked out really well because they developed an avid following for the Red Wings on both sides of the border. Most of the players in those days were Canadians.

Jack, he had ideas. Adams picked the Soo because the players could come across the border there easily and they wouldn't be near their family for 8-10 days. He insisted that after practice in the morning, the guys go and play 18 holes of golf. Well, only about five of us played golf - Gordie Howe, myself, Ted Lindsay, trainer Lefty Wilson and Jimmy Peters. But the reason he wanted them all to go and play golf and walk 18 holes was that meant for three-and-a-half-hours, they wouldn't be in a bar.

I believe that a lot of the Michiganders who went on to become prominent NHLers, such as Mike Modano, Pat LaFontaine and the Hatcher and Miller families, they owe some small piece of their success to the legacy of Jack Adams because he was the man who sold the state on the beauty of the game of hockey. He planted the seeds that allowed Detroit to blossom as Hockeytown.

He went to banquets everywhere across the state and to kids hockey games. He couldn't wait to go out and encourage other people to get involved in hockey. He'd take members of the team on a whirlwind tour of Michigan every year. He sold the sport. He was a firm believer that it had to be sold.

Adams loved to entertain and one of his favorite entertainers and good friends was the great Canadian bandleader Guy Lombardo. One of Jack's favorite spots every trip to New York was to take all the broadcasters and the beat writers out on the town. We'd have to go to wherever Guy Lombardo was playing. And as soon as we'd walk into the ballroom, no matter what song was playing or whether people were dancing, Guy would see that Jack had come in and he'd stop the music and play "Pretty Red Wing" for Jack. In Windsor, Jack's sister went to a church where Lombardo was one time, and Jack was also in Windsor that day and was invited to the house to meet him. That's how the friendship began.

Jack never forgot the key people in his life and yet he was humble enough to be around everyday people. When he went to the Windsor Arena, Jack would never sit in the press box. He'd always go up and sit in the corner. He wanted to sit in the stands. He knew the fans would yell at him, but he loved it. He needed it.

Jack had bird dogs everywhere. Carson Cooper, a former NHL player and a Hamilton boy I knew from way back, was one of his key scouts. Coop would hang around amateur hockey in Hamilton and Toronto and all parts of Ontario. And that's when he found Ted Lindsay and Red Kelly at St. Mike's and Marty Pavelich in Sault Ste. Marie.

Adams had loyal people working for him. At one time, Montreal's credo was that any French-Canadian boy had to go to Montreal first. Jack Adams knew a writer in Montreal and the writer had a boy who was a pretty good hockey player and Jack made arrangements for the kid to come and join the Windsor Spitfires, Detroit's junior affiliate in the Ontario Hockey Association. He was a goalie. At that time, Jack had the pipeline. He was getting people who wanted to come play in the Detroit system.

Jack, in his own way, was a very unique individual. He was a diehard baseball nut. He couldn't wait to go to the games. He got to know Ty Tyson, who was broadcasting the Detroit Tigers games at the time. I think Adams knew legendary Tigers slugger Ty Cobb from the way he talked about him. Former Tigers first baseman Harry Heilmann -- another member of the club's broadcast team at the time -- lived in Dearborn when I lived there, and I got to know Harry pretty well because he was doing baseball back then. Jack had his own outlook on life about certain things and it was self-evident from the greatness of Red Wings' teams under him right from the start that he was tough.

Jack was under the Norris regime in Detroit. There's no doubt about it that even when Jack Adams became the general manager, he still had that control of being able to get to the players. I think we've lost that link today. The agents are involved and it's much different.

There's no doubt that Adams was a man who was set in his crusty, old ways. It's quite true that after many a game, he'd come out of the building and get in the car with his wife Helen and they'd drive for half an hour, just trying to unwind. He didn't want to talk to anybody when he lost.

At Red Wings' home games in Olympia Stadium, Helen Adams sat behind the visitor's bench with a couple of priests from Ontario. Some of the visiting teams, they'd say, "Be careful what you say. Jack Adams' spy is right behind you."

He had such a competitive way, if the Red Wings at the old Olympia say lost to Montreal 7-1, the players could not go out the back door of the dressing room. They had to walk down the passageway by the visitor's dressing room, right down the corridor where all the press and fans would be gathered. And the fans were right there behind the wooden barriers. They wanted to see you up close and they might yell at you if they wanted. He made the players face the music, and I think little things like that were worthwhile in developing a winning attitude within the team.

I'm sure that behind the scenes, Jack Adams respected loyalty. He demanded it from his team. Loyalty to the Red Wings and a complete focus on being the best player you could be for the team was a 12-month a year, seven-days a week, 24-hour pursuit in his mind.

Glen Skov was a tall, lanky kid, a checking forward who was part of three Stanley Cup winners with Detroit in the 1950s. Skov was part of a great hockey family. Art Skov, his brother, had a fabulous career of his own as an NHL referee. Well, Glen Skov and George Armstrong, captain for the Toronto Maple Leafs, got involved in a mishap one night. Going along the boards, Army kicked at the puck and caught Skov right in the Achilles heel. It punctured the skate.

The next spring, back out behind Olympia Stadium, they had three or four baseball stadiums. Well, Adams came out to watch some ball one day and who does he see but Skov, playing for the Detroit Fire Department. Skov got a single and scored. When he crossed home plate, Adams was waiting from him and he said, "Take those spikes off and if you ever play baseball again, you'll never put a Red Wings sweater on again." He didn't want him to aggravate the foot sliding around a muddy field, so Skov gave up his baseball career.

Then there's the story of Gord Haidy. There's a kid that could have made it, who should have made it. Haidy was down in Indianapolis, with Detroit's American Hockey League farm club and Jack had Haidy come up for a game on a Sunday. Haidy gets into the railway station in the afternoon and goes right to the Olympia. Lefty was there getting the gear ready for the game and Gord tells him, "I left my skates in my locker in Indianapolis." Lefty says, "Don't worry, we'll get you some skates." Well, the story gets back to Adams. Haidy sat by the bench, never got on the ice and afterwards, Jack handed him return railway tickets to Indianapolis, because he believed Haidy had been irresponsible in not remembering his skates. In those days, players had to travel with their own skates. You carried your skates with you all of the time. After a game in Maple Leaf Gardens, every night, when we would go by the Toronto dressing room, you'd see all the skates laid out. Some skates were going to Rochester, Toronto's farm team, some were going with the Leafs.

That being said, Jack also had a soft spot. I had a friend, Jim Parise, who operated Arrow Salvage in Eastern Market. He would take the damaged food -- vegetables, soup, etc. -- from the trains at the station. Then Jack would take canned goods to the convents and ask the nuns to, "Pray for us. We've got to play Montreal."

I'll tell another story about what happened at training camp one year. He's calling the players in one at a time to sign them to their contracts. At the time, everybody said, "Get in there before Gordie (Howe), or there won't be anything left on the table." Well, Gordie wasn't making that much money, either. Normie Ullman's wife Bibs, she made Normie, when he came to training camp that year, bring a slip of paper with what he wanted. So when Normie got called in, written on the back of an envelope, Bibs had penciled in, "If he gets five more goals than last year, he gets a $500 bonus. If he gets 10 more assists than last year, he gets a $500 bonus. If we win the league, he gets a $500 bonus." She had five different $500 bonus clauses written down. Jack was sitting there and says, "Oh, by all means, Normie, by all means. You've got $2,500 in potential bonus money. Good luck on that." Then he just signed him to an inexpensive contract.

That Christmas, Normie was flat. He couldn't put the puck in the open net. And Adams, who was pretty crafty, went to Bibs. He called her into the office one day and said, "I've got to tell you something, Mrs. Ullman. In training camp, you got me to agree to $2,500 in potential bonus money for April, the end of the season. I think you've blown it all. You better talk to him." Well, Normie came back the second half of the year and had one of his best years.

The incentive thing is what makes a player conscious of the fact there's more money to be made by getting more goals, getting more assists, winning more games, getting through the first round of the playoffs. Those are the things that kept competitive hockey alive in the 1950s and 1960s. And then the incentive was lost when they put the money up front. They'll give a guy a contract who has never played a pro game and he's making more money than some of the guys already established as players in the league.

I don't know whether Jack would have survived complete expansion. There were so many fringe players who came in when the World Hockey Association started. When Winnipeg took Bobby Hull from Chicago in 1972 and offered him a million-dollar contract that was the end of player loyalty to owners. Boy from then on that dollar sign got to be so important.

Jack was a tough one to negotiate with, there's no doubt about that. Among themselves, some guys would bemoan the fact that they're not making much money, they're not getting enough ice time because the coach Tommy Ivan decided to bench them and make them suffer. Well, he'd hear stories. I'm sure Jack heard them second-hand, but he heard them. Well, those things started to fester a little bit and sure, some of it was true, because many a time, you'd wonder why a guy was sitting on the bench. But it was about getting even, too.

Then when the trades took place, oh boy. I think of Terry Sawchuk going to Boston after the Stanley Cup in 1955. Adams traded the winning team away one year to Chicago. Whether he felt he owed the Blackhawks a favor because of the Norris-Wirtz tie-in between the families, which owned the two teams, or he resented certain players, I don't know for sure. And directly, Ted Lindsay will say to this day that after he got involved with trying to get a union started in 1957, Adams dealt him to Chicago out of spite.

And then Gordie Howe, of course, was Adams' man and Ted always felt that if Gordie had gone along with him, they would have got it started. But Gordie was a Western boy, a quiet guy and he didn't want to get involved, didn't really understand unions. And when the trading started, it was like a revolving door. Every time you turned around, somebody else was going to Boston; somebody else was going to Chicago.

When he decided to get rid of all those guys, it was lock, stock and barrel after such a successful run that was it for the Wings. Remember, there were only six teams at the time. Detroit was right there with Montreal and Toronto, but from then on, it was rebuild the machine, rebuild the machine.

I think that Jack's demise, a lot of it has to go back to those trades. Some of the players, Lindsay especially, think that's where it started. Team unity was lost. When you can ship out guys like Ted, Johnny Wilson, Sawchuk, key people who made the team in those good years, it made a big difference in the dressing room.

When it came time in 1962, I won't mention certain names of people in the building, but they were involved, I know that for sure. Sid Abel, who was coaching the Wings at the time, and I went up to a restaurant on Grand River and Sid said, "I'm going to get a call here and I've got to go back up to the building for a meeting. I think they're going to fire me." And the weird thing was that Sid's wife Gloria Abel had been Jack Adams's secretary from way back. Anyway, Sid gets the phone call, so I stayed in the restaurant and had lunch. He called me about an hour later and he said, "Budd, I've got Gloria coming up to the office if you want to stop in." I said, "What happened?" Sid said, "I got into the room, (president and chairman) Bruce Norris, (vice-president) Linc Cavalieri and Jack Adams were there and Norris came out and said right away, "Jack, we want you to retire. You've done a great job for us, for the family, for hockey in general, but you're at that stage where we want you to retire." Jack was stubborn. "I'm not going to retire," he said. So the other choice was let him go. He went out the door and Norris turns to Sid and says, "You're acting general manager." Sid thought he was going to get axed and here he is, acting general manager. He didn't know what to think. An hour later, he went to Jack's office and all the files were gone. Adams had taken that hour to take every one of his files. Sid said afterwards, "What the heck was he going to do with the files?" He just didn't want them to have anything left to work with. So Sid inherited the job and NHL president Clarence Campbell and the league were upset with the fact that Jack was let go.

Jack's health went downhill and Helen wasn't well either and that's when they decided to put him in as the titular head of the new Central Professional Hockey League. But he had a tough time trying to weather the adjustment, working out of an office in East Detroit. It wasn't the same. He wasn't going to where the players were and he didn't know the guys in these other cities. It was sad.

But business is business. It gets ruthless after a while. Being let go by Detroit, it took the life out of Jack, though. Literally. He died of a heart attack right at his desk in that office on May 1, 1968.

One thing I must tell you about Jack. Clarence Campbell called me after Jack had passed away. He said, "I want to have a Jack Adams Trophy." The idea was that the award would recognize the top coach in the NHL each year. With the help of some trophy-design personnel in Detroit, we created a trophy which was highlighted by an old photo of Jack in his button-down Red Wings sweater that he wore on the ice all of the time, the typical garb of coaches at practices during his era.

The Jack Adams Award is presented annually by the NHL Broadcasters' Association to the coach adjudged to have contributed the most to his team's success. It was first presented in 1974 and it's been won four times by Red Wings coaches: Bobby Kromm (1978), Jacques Demers (1987 and 1988) and Scotty Bowman (1996). Bowman was also a finalist for the honor in 1995 and 2001.

It's a fitting tribute to the man who gave so much to the game of hockey.

The Wings I Knew

CHAPTER SIX

❝ *You were together more when there were only six teams."*

- Budd Lynch

My first experience around National Hockey League players - well, future National Hockey League players that is -- came while I was growing up in Hamilton.

Playing as a juvenile, we scrimmaged against the Hamilton seniors. They had some great players on that team -- Maxie Bennett, Gonie McGowan, Toe Blake and a kid from McMaster University named Syl Apps. He was a tall, skinny kid.

Both Blake and Apps went to enjoy Hall of Fame careers and became two of the most famous icons in Canadian hockey history. Blake broke in with the Montreal Maroons in 1934-35, but after just eight games, they traded him to their cross-town rivals, the Canadiens. With Montreal he became a superstar, playing left wing on the famous Punch Line alongside center Elmer Lach and right-winger Maurice (Rocket) Richard. He was a five-time NHL All-Star selection, led the NHL in scoring in 1938-39 and won the Hart Trophy as the league's MVP that season. And do you know who was runner-up in the balloting that season? Apps, that's who. Blake also won the Lady Byng Trophy in 1945-46.

Blake won three Stanley Cups with the Canadiens as a player, but his true legendary status was fashioned behind the Montreal bench. He took over as coach of the team at the start of the 1955-56 season and won the Stanley Cup in his first five seasons at the helm of the team, a record that will likely never be matched. He won eight Stanley Cups in 13 years as Montreal's coach. Many people in the game consider Scotty Bowman to be the greatest coach in hockey history, but if you ask Scotty, he'll tell you it was Toe.

Apps was a tremendous athlete at Hamilton's McMaster University, and a lot of people don't know that he competed in the pole vault for Canada at the 1936 Summer Olympic Games in Germany. Apps captained the Toronto Maple Leafs to three Stanley Cups, won the Calder Trophy in 1936-37, the Lady Byng Trophy in 1941-42 and was a four-time NHL All-Star choice.

Apps was a wonderful gentleman, first class in every way. He served as an elected official in the Ontario government after his retirement from hockey. That was interesting, because getting into broadcasting, I got a chance to follow his career. What a credit to hockey he was.

I don't think I ever got involved in hero worshiping and didn't really root for a specific team and maybe that helped a lot when I entered broadcasting because you can't be opinionated. You shouldn't be anyway. Maybe it was the influence of being around such great players at a young age and realizing that they were no different people than the rest of us.

Certainly, once I landed the play-by-play job in Detroit, that was how I looked upon the Red Wings players. I didn't idolize them, but I definitely respected them.

During the days of the Original Six, the competition between teams, because you saw so much of each other, was intense. Every city had character hockey players. Hard-working grinders like Tony Leswick, Marty Pavelich and Glen Skov, who frequently played in checking roles, their desire was to improve on what they did in the previous game against the same team. I think inwardly, that's when a hockey player develops. He's not afraid of a guy like Montreal defenseman Butch Bouchard. He's not afraid of a big guy like that. He wants to check the guy who got him the last time. I don't think it carries on that way today, the rivalry between teams and individual players, because there's too fast of a change.

I believe that train travel had a lot to do with the closeness of the players in that era. You were together more when there were only six teams. Now, you wonder. The few times I've traveled the last few years as a guest of the team, when you hit a city, there's agents there, there's lawyers there. The veterans don't take the rookies out, and the rookies are lost in some of these cities. One thing about the Red Wings over the years, they always have a team meal where everybody eats together at the same place. But you wonder how are you ever going to get back to that way?

They go to so many different places in all parts of North America and every city has its attractions. Nowadays, I notice that as soon as that bus arrives from the airport to the hotels, the players, they scatter. They're just gone. You wonder where they're going. They can't have that many relatives.

In the old days, traveling by train, the players would wait to hear general manager Jack Adams snoring in his compartment and coach Tommy Ivan snoring in his compartment ,and then they would crack open their beer bottles. They'd recall the game, because usually, they were going to be playing the same team the next night in Detroit, and if they were embarrassed in Montreal, boy they couldn't wait to nail those guys.

The lower berth guys - Terry Sawchuk, Bob Goldham, Red Kelly and Gordie Howe and Ted Lindsay, these were the guys who were taking care of the rookies. "Don't be intimidated," they'd say. "Hit those Frenchmen." A back-to-back series, one game would be played in Montreal, Canadiens style, and the next night in Detroit, it would be Red Wings style. It made for an interesting rivalry.

The Canadiens sleeper car would be right behind our car and you had to go through the Red Wings car to get to the diner. The diner car was put on board just outside of Toronto and breakfast would be served between 7-8 o'clock. This one time - Lindsay was the instigator of it - He said, "I'm going to fix those Frenchmen today." Ted was always very outspoken about what he wanted to do. He had five guys get up at 6:30 and go to the dining car and he put one guy at each table. There was no room for anybody else but the Red Wings. The Canadiens didn't get their breakfast until about 9:30 that morning and boy were they mad. Adams caught hell for it, but the players would never admit who did it.

The players got very little in terms of money when they won the Stanley Cup back then. The Downriver fans, many of them ex-Canadians - The Gorno family who were big car dealers, Stu Evans, who was an ex-Red Wings player and also a car dealer - these fans would have a big party at Grosse Ile Country Club. One year they gave us gift certificates from Hudson's. Another year, they gave us Blazers. The last year, 1954-55, Milkin Jewellers designed a ring with the Red Wings logo and a sapphire and gave one to every player, wife and all of the trainers and broadcasters. There was a real togetherness with the Downriver fans.

Every player on the team was supremely talented and unique in his own special way.

Terry Sawchuk was a loner. He had his own way of doing things, but boy he was tough. Whenever we had a close game in Montreal, by the time I'd come down from the broadcast booth to the dressing room, he was the last guy to shower and he'd give me the high sign when he came out. He'd call me over and he'd want me to sit with him because he didn't want the writers to come over and interview him. One time, Jacques Beauchamp, one of the French-language newspaper writers, he said to me, "What were you

Zebra or jailbird? My stripes are going the wrong way as I work as an official during a Red Wings alumni game at Olympia Stadium.

Just call me the long arm of the law. I went with a Keystone Cops outfit, while Detroit media personality and longtime friend Sonny Eliot employed a slighty oversized goal stick during a charity event at Olympia Stadium in 1954.

guys talking about?" "We were talking about our golf game next week," I told him. Eventually, they got wise to it, that Sawchuk didn't want to be interviewed.

Sawchuk hurt his arm in baseball when he was growing up in Winnipeg and he had a shriveled arm. One year we were playing Chicago and owner Bruce Norris took the whole team to a resort area they had outside the city with a swimming pool and everything else. We were in the water and talking about diving off the low board. Gordie Howe says, "I'm like a pencil when I go in the water." So I said, "I want to see Sawchuk go in there with his one wing up in the air." It ending up evolving into a diving competition among the players. I told Pit Martin, "I'm betting on you." And he said, "You'd better." "He can't dive," someone said. I told Pit I had bets on him with five different guys and he said, "How much do I get?" "Half," I told him. That was one time where my Hamilton background paid off. Pit Martin was on the diving and swimming team at Hamilton's McMaster University when he was in school. I knew about that.

Sawchuk was an unbelievably talented netminder. People thought Jack Adams was crazy in the summer of 1950 when he traded Harry Lumley to Chicago, right after he'd backstopped Detroit to the Stanley Cup. But Sawchuk silenced the critics quickly. He was the NHL's top rookie in 1950-51 and turned in the most impressive goaltending performance in the history of the Stanley Cup the following spring, going 8-0 with four shutouts, a brilliant 0.63 goals-against average and an astounding .977 save percentage as he led the Wings to the Stanley Cup.

Sawchuk became the only goalie to start his NHL career and post a GAA under 2.00 in each of his first five seasons. He led the NHL in wins in every one of those campaigns and posted 56 of his NHL-record 103 shutouts in that span.

Every team was backed by an outstanding goaltender in those days and you wondered when you saw them, how they survived, facing all those shots without wearing a mask to protect their faces. There were only six teams and no back-up goalie back then, so that meant six jobs were up for grabs, so you really had to be some kind of quality puckstopper to gain regular work in the NHL.

Montreal had Jacques Plante and the New York Rangers had Charlie

Rayner and later, Gump Worsley. Rayner, he was a great baseball player, a catcher. Some of his maneuvers in the net, that glove was always out there like a catcher. Rayner was a big athlete and he sure kept them in there. The Rangers were never a great team in the 1950s. We had little goalies who could eat the rubber. An acrobatic guy like Detroit's Roger Crozier, I think his head hit the crossbar most of the time, he was so small. Sawchuk with the shriveled arm, he could only go one way at one time and he developed that low crouch of his to help him cover the bottom of the net on his glove side. Johnny Bower came out of the American Hockey League to join Toronto and he knew how to cut the angle down, one of the first you ever saw. It was sound strategy because if you don't give a guy enough area to shoot at, he's going to shoot at you.

Sawchuk used to say, "I need five more defensemen to stack the blue-line, and I can make 20 saves a night." Because then, all the shots would come from outside the blue-line and his life would be a pretty easy one.

Detroit certainly had its share of stalwart defensemen. You had Benny Woit, who was rock-solid and Bob Goldham, who was a masterful shot blocker, maybe the best ever. And Marcel Pronovost, who was an unsung hero his whole career. Marcel was kind of overlooked with Red Kelly on the team, but he won five Stanley Cups -- four of them with Detroit -- and was a four-time All-Star selection, who played 11 NHL All-Star Games, and was inducted into the Hockey Hall of Fame in 1978. He's still winning Stanley Cups as a scout with the New Jersey Devils. He's getting recognition now and that's great to see. The Windsor Spitfires, where Marcel played his junior hockey, recently honored his number in a ceremony at Windsor Arena. He did everything so well because he worked at it so hard, including language. He was frustrated like Gordie Howe was, not having an education, but they worked at it together. I'm still not sure how Jack Adams got such a talented French-Canadian player out of Quebec right out from under the watchful eyes of the Montreal Canadiens scouts. Montreal got all of the top French-Canadian players back then and it made the Habs a dynamic and unique team. I don't know if we'll ever see again a true French-Canadian hockey team like we saw in Montreal.

Red Kelly was a quiet leader, indirectly. He's one of two defensemen in NHL history to win the Lady Byng as the league's most sportsmanlike player -- Detroit's Bill Quackenbush was the other -- and he won it four times. He was also the first winner of the Norris Trophy, which was introduced in 1953-54 to recognize the NHL's top defenseman. He won eight Stanley Cups -- four in Detroit and four in Toronto, where Leafs coach Punch Imlach amazingly converted Red into a center. Red was selected to eight All-Star teams and played in 13 NHL All-Star Games.

One of my claims to fame was that I stood up for him when he got married to his wife Andra, who was a figure skater. Red came from a tobacco farm and Jack Adams used to take the team down there for a fund raiser for the church, but we had to get rid of Jack because there was beer around. Red's uncle would always take Jack for a tour of the other tobacco farms to give us a little freedom to enjoy ourselves.

Red Kelly roomed with Eddie Shack in Toronto. Eddie Shack couldn't read or write. Red kept on him, "Learn how to do your initials. Once you get that, you'll be able to move on to the word Eddie and then Shack" and eventually, Eddie learned to write his name. Shack was one of the Maple Leafs' most popular players with the fan base there, and they named a horse after Shack in Toronto, a thoroughbred. They made a big deal out of it in the Toronto papers. So they go down to the barn area with some newspaper photographers. They didn't call him Shack, they had a nickname for him, "Clear The Track," because that was the way he skated, too. The horse, they had it in a stall and the horse hit both walls. So then Shack did the same thing and the next day in the papers, they had pictures of Shack hitting both walls. They also called him, "The Entertainer" and he was an entertainer, all right.

Of course, no story of the Red Wings of that era would be complete without discussion of the legendary Production Line - Sid Abel in the middle, with Gordie Howe on the right wing and Ted Lindsay on the left side. All three of them are in the Hall of Fame, a rarity for an entire forward line.

When they made the Production Line, it was a perfect marriage of hockey talent - the veteran Sid, Ted the competitor and Gordie the utopia of thinking and mind. Gordie had all the potential an the ability of doing everything. Adams' foresight of putting the three of them together was a stroke of genius. Sid Abel, late in his career, used to tell stories on himself.

"I'd just tell those two kids what to do," he'd say. "I'd get as far as the blue-line. If I get to the red line, it's going in the corner. One of you two guys go and get it." He'd tell me he got 10 goals every year just by staying in front of the net.

Sid was one of the few NHLers to be named to the All-Star Team at two different positions - at left wing (1941-42) and center (1949, 1950, 1951). Both Sid and Gordie won Hart Trophies as MVPs of the NHL. Sid got his in 1949 and Gordie won the award a half dozen times. Between them, the Production Line captured seven MVP awards, seven scoring titles, six playoff scoring crowns, led the NHL in goal scoring seven times, were selected 22 times to the NHL First All-Star Team, 12 times to the Second All-Star Team and combined to appear in 37 NHL All-Star Games. In 1949-50, they finished 1-2-3 in the NHL scoring race -- Lindsay (78 points), followed by Abel (69) and Howe (69).

Ted, whose father Bert was a goalie with the Montreal Wanderers in 1917-18, the NHL's first season, was the most competitive player I ever saw in action. He could do it all, leading the league in scoring in 1949-50 and in penalty minutes in 1958-59. He was a born leader and both he and Sid captained Detroit to Stanley Cup championships during their careers. He was part of four Stanley Cup winners and is the only Red Wings player to score four goals in a Stanley Cup game. He did that against Montreal in the 1955 final, and he also changed the way teams celebrated Stanley Cup wins that spring. NHL president Clarence Campbell made the announcement congratulating the Wings and an excited Ted scooped up the Cup off the table and held it over his head. In 1964-65, he ended a four-year retirement and scored 14 goals with the Wings at the age of 39. Ted was a nine-time All-Star who played in 11 NHL All-Star Games and like Sid, he later became coach and GM of the Wings.

Sid Abel was another character in our travels. I had so much fun with him. The unfortunate thing was that in his era, the Production Line, they were so impressive to everybody and when Sid moved up the ladder as general manager and coach, everyone expected the same brilliance, but the Wings were a declining club by the time Sid took over. I think it was tough for him to go from a player to the boss of the players. He invariably would stay in the bar in the hotel. He had a theory and it was pretty good one, too.

One night, we're playing at Madison Square Garden and Sid said, "Boy, if we could ever beat the Rangers here, that would really be something," and we did that night, 4-1. By the time I got downstairs to the bar, he said, "I can't wait to have that first one." We were staying at the Piccadilly Hotel, about a 20-minute walk from the Garden. Sid had a deal with the players. If he was in the bar, they don't come in. If any players were in the bar, he wouldn't come in. So as a prank, 15 players staggered themselves through the first five bars from Madison Square Garden up to Fifth Avenue. They did it on purpose. We had to walk five blocks to get to a bar to have our first celebratory drink.

They called him Bootnose and there's a funny story about how he got the title. Gordie had just come up to the big club and the Rocket took a run at him in the Forum. Sid came over and said, "Don't you do that to our pride and joy," and the Rocket popped him one right in the beak.

Bruce Norris named one of his racehorses after Sid and called it Bootnose. One night we went to see him race. He had a big blanket on him that said Bootnose. Sid posed with the horse for pictures.

Getting mixed up with the Rocket that night was one of the few wrong turns Sid ever made on the ice. He'd learn soon that big Gord didn't require protection. He could take care of himself.

In fact, there wasn't anything that Gordie couldn't do in a hockey rink, except maybe sit on the bench.

You're A Great One Mr. Howe

CHAPTER SEVEN

❝ *He was the heir apparent, even when he was young."*

- Budd Lynch

I saw more of Gordie Howe, perhaps, than anybody else. I saw him put on his jock more than anybody else. Gordie was just one of those rarities. The Wings really stole him. When Jack Adams brought him in to play for the Windsor Spitfires, he'd already brought two imports from outside the area in for the team, so he had to put Gordie in Galt for awhile.

The first time I met him, he was a 16-year-old kid coming from Western Canada. Gordie was born in Floral, Saskatchewan, just outside of Saskatoon, and I'd see him at the practice sessions with the Spitfires and later when he was with the organization. He was the heir apparent even then when he was young. You knew Gordie was going to be something special from the first moment you saw him on the ice. When I saw him play a couple of pre-season games, it was clearly evident he was destined for greatness. He wanted to be on the ice 60 minutes and it wasn't easy to keep him off the ice. He had strength in his moves. He was a farm boy that grew up working hard. I don't think they knew what weightlifting was in those days. Gordie's favorite phrase used to be, "I've got no shoulders." As a kid, he carried cement bags for his dad, so he had these sloping shoulders. I think it boiled down to the ability to put the skates on every day and practice, practice, practice. That's what Gordie did. He did extra skating time. When I think of the number of times that Gordie would go and suit-up just to practice, on top of playing a 70-game season it's truly impressive. That's another character trait all of the great ones possess -- no matter what sport they play – they have that unending desire to improve their game.

Gordie was appreciative of being able to play a sport he loved, even though he had no education. Fortunately, he was around Sid Abel and Ted Lindsay to form the Production Line to get started, but Gordie in his own right, was always Gordie Howe. The opposition feared him. He was accused of using the elbows and his forearm when the referee wasn't looking. Well, more power to the guy if you can get away with it. Gordie's physique was just amazing. Ted Lindsay was another who was always in shape, but Gordie was strong. You wouldn't dare go in the corner with him. He'd not only have you out of the play, but he'd have the puck and you'd be on the ice. He was challenged by some of the big bruisers around the league. Emile (Butch) Bouchard in Montreal, he used to love to nail him. And he'd get him once in a while, but Gordie would get up and laugh at him. Next time behind the net, when Bouchard got caught back there, he was the one who was on the ice.

He was respected around the league. There are certain players, smart hockey players, who know when a guy is going to run them. Ted Lindsay got traded to Chicago in 1956. When Detroit and the Blackhawks played the first game against each other during the 1956-57 season, the first time they met behind the net in the Chicago end, Lindsay took Gordie into the boards pretty hard. Gordie very quickly said, "Want to play it that way Teddy?" The next shift on the ice, he caught Lindsay right away with a stiff bodycheck.

A great story about Gordie Howe. He wore 17 when he first came up from Omaha of the United States League for 1946-47, his first NHL season. The following season, Carl Mattson, the trainer, said, "Roy Conacher got traded to the New York Rangers and Gord, you're going to wear No. 9 this season." Gordie said, "No, No, I like 17. I'm just pleased to have a Red Wings' sweater." And Carl said, "You're going to wear No. 9, because then you'll have a lower berth on the train." And that's why Gordie first took No. 9.

Gordie did everything well. He was an outstanding fisherman. One thing he loved – and he was a pretty good at it – was baseball. He'd often take batting practice with the Detroit Tigers and wow the fans by driving a few balls over the fences at Tiger Stadium. We'd sit on the bus together and in hotel lobbies. We'd work on crossword puzzles together and he always admitted to me that he was sorry he hadn't gone further in school. In those days, if you wanted to play hockey, you had to leave home at a young age. Your education was self-education. Marcel Pronovost was another player who would sit with me on the bus a lot of the time, working crossword puzzles, to try and learn more English. Marcel and Gordie would work on crossword puzzles together. Marcel would help Gordie with the French words in the crossword puzzles and Gordie would help Marcel with the English words.

Gordie scored a goal in his first NHL game on Oct. 16, 1946. Sid Abel won the draw and Gordie snapped a shot past Hall of Famer Turk Broda in a 3-3 tie against Toronto. Later in that game, he laid out Toronto's Syl Apps with a devastating bodycheck that put the Leafs captain out of the game. In his third game, Gordie touched off a brawl when he steamrolled Chicago goalie Paul Bibeault. He was quickly establishing that he could do it all on the ice. Adams called Gordie the best prospect he'd seen in 20 years.

He'd jumped right from the low minor leagues, the United States League, past the American League and directly into the NHL at the age of 18, which was unheard of in those days. As talented as he was, Gordie, like all rookies in the six-team era, had to earn his stripes and spent a lot of time on the bench that first season, finishing with seven goals.

In 1947-48, Detroit coach Tommy Ivan first formed the famous Production Line of Sid Abel, Ted Lindsay and Gordie. They combined for 66 goals in 1948-49 and Abel won the Hart Trophy as MVP. They really blossomed as a unit during the 1949-50 season, my first season doing the Wings play-by-play. Gordie scored 35 goals that season, equaling his combined output for his first three NHL campaigns. At six-feet tall and 201-pounds, Gordie was the prototype of what's known today as the power forward. He could beat you with his skill or his size.

That was the year that he got hurt. That was as close to an athlete's career coming to an end as I'd seen. It was against Toronto in the first game of the 1950 Stanley Cup playoffs. It happened so quickly, a collision between Gordie and Toronto captain Teeder Kennedy. You saw it happen close to the bench, but you didn't know what it was that had happened. They had a knob on the end of their sticks in those days and it's not too often that they'd use it on each other. Usually they'd just give you a little of the forearm.

It was a stick in the side of the head. You could see that by the reaction from the Red Wings' bench. Gordie went into the boards and Teeder Kennedy -- there's no way of ever saying that a guy did anything deliberately -- but those butt ends they had on hockey sticks in those days, they'd catch you in the ribs with them. It was one of the old tricks. But to come up that high, there was no doubt he was off-balance and that it was unintentional. I've always said that. Teeder Kennedy admitted later on that he was off-balance when they collided. He told me, "I took him into the boards and his head bounced and hit the end of my stick." They talked about it later on, Teeder and Gordie. Now, Teeder -- there was a competitor for Toronto. They'd go wild at Maple Leaf Gardens whenever he came on the ice. All you could hear in the building was, "Come on, Teeder."

Gordie was carried off the ice and taken to the hospital and Jack Adams spent the whole night in the hospital room with him. When Gordie was in the hospital that night and the next day, we got the reports and they were pretty grim at first. The doctors did a great thing. They put a small hole the size of about a quarter in the side of his skull and drained the fluid off of the brain to ensure there was no brain damage. There was no damage to the brain itself, only the skull was damaged. It was touch-and-go there for awhile, but Gordie was as strong as he was tough and he pulled through.

The team really rallied after Gordie's injury. Both playoff series that spring went seven games and each time, the Wings battled back from 3-2 series deficits to take the round, winning both Game 7 contests in overtime. Leo Reise scored the winner against Toronto, his second OT winner of the series, and Pete Babando turning the trick in double OT in the final against the New York Rangers. For Gordie to be on the ice in his street clothes, when the championship ended a few weeks later and the Stanley Cup was presented to the Wings, it was a site to remember, total bedlam. When he came out on the ice as the Cup was brought out by NHL President Clarence Campbell, oh the crowd went absolutely wild.

Gordie was a question mark the next year. Jack Adams just hoped he'd be able to skate. He would go and skate on his own, just to get the feel of his legs under him again. He had to wear a so-called helmet, a soft-leather helmet.

It turned out that Gordie was just beginning his level of dominance of the NHL, a level never before seen. He marked his return from the injury by leading the NHL in scoring in 1950-51, setting a new NHL record for points (86) while leading the league in both goals (43) and assists (45). He was the first player to do so since Howie Morenz of the Montreal Canadiens in 1927-28. Gordie tied his mark with another 86 points in 1951-52, then set a new NHL points mark of 95 in 1952-53, winning his third successive scoring title in the process. Gordie also scored 49 goals that season, which would stand as the Red Wings' single-season record until 1972-73. There would be a fourth straight scoring title for Howe in 1953-54. To that point in NHL history, no other player had ever topped the league in scoring for more than two seasons in succession.

They loved Gordie like no other Detroit athlete had ever been loved. At the Olympia, one time, the fans honored him and they arranged for a station wagon with the license plate GH9999 to be brought out on the ice to be presented to him during the ceremony, but there was a twist. In honoring him, his mother Katherine had not been well, and his dad Ab was up in years. Air Canada flew them in from Saskatoon, but Gordie was unaware of this. I had come down from the broadcast booth to handle the ceremonies and present the keys to Gordie. Before I handed him the keys, I was to open the back door and there in the back seat were his mom and dad. Gordie broke down, but why wouldn't he? They were his mom and dad. He tried to make a speech, but he couldn't say anything, he was so choked-up with emotion. That was a great tribute that night.

The fans loved Gordie and opponents respected him because he could do it all on the ice. If you needed a big goal, he could score it or make the play to create it. He could work as a checker, briefly played defense for the Wings in the 1970s, and when it came to toughness, he was the NHL's undisputed heavyweight champion. Most players were smart enough not to mess with Gordie because they knew they'd suffer the consequences. For those foolish enough to get Gordie's dander up, they usually regretted it. He was the king of payback. Just ask Lou Fontinato.

I'm broadcasting from the old Madison Square Garden on Feb. 1, 1959. I thought I was Don Dunphy, the old fight announcer. New York Rangers defenseman Fontinato fancied himself to be the toughest guy in the league. And he was a tough hockey player. He'd led the NHL in penalty minutes with a record 202 in 1955-56, and was atop the bad man list again in 1957-58. I can see to this day, Lou coming from his defensive zone, dropping a glove, getting up to center ice, dropping the other glove and he has no stick in his hands by now. He gets to Detroit's defensive zone and Gordie's got his skate caught in the mesh in the back part of the net. In comes Lou and he's like a charging bull. Gordie senses there's going to be an uppercut, so Gordie ducks and sure enough, here comes the uppercut. And with that, Gordie gets his skate free. Detroit's Billy McNeill was the guy who originally caused the trouble behind the net, but Lou's going to take on Gordie. It would be good publicity for New York, you know. Now, Gordie gets his skate caught again and his head's down, but Lou has his head down too, so Gordie uppercuts him. And Gordie was strong enough to let both arms go and boy, did Gordie ever start to flail away and you could see the blood splashing. Afterwards, Dr. Nardiello, the doctor at Madison Square Garden for the fights, wrestling and hockey, kept Lou Fontinato in his room until everyone was out of the Garden. His nose was over on one cheekbone; the cheekbone was fractured; the orbital bone was fractured, and there were blood vessels ruptured. Luckily, the hospital was right down the street from the old Madison Square Garden. A Life Magazine photographer was in there because his wife was having a baby and he happened to snap a picture of Lou, and that became a classic. The magazine did a three-page spread of the carnage to Lou's face. What a mess. Lou and Gordie talked about it several times afterwards, but Lou was never the same after that. It was just one of those things. If Gordie had been free, I don't know if there would have been any blows thrown. He tried to get away from the net, but he couldn't.

Through his whole career, Gordie was an entity unto himself. No one else had done what he was doing and no one has equaled his unparalleled accomplishments since. Between 1948-49 and 1969-70, he was selected to the NHL's First or Second All-Star Teams every season except 1954-55, when Montreal Canadiens right-wingers Bernie Geoffrion and Rocket Richard finished 1-2 in NHL scoring. But Gordie got the last laugh, tallying the Stanley Cup-winning goal as the Wings defeated Montreal in a seven-game series. He was an ever-present in the NHL's top 10 scorers from 1949-50 through 1969-70, an NHL record. He captured six scoring titles and six Hart Trophies as NHL MVP. Howe played in a record 23 NHL All-Star Games. Gordie and Mark Messier are the only players in NHL history who rank in the top 10 in career games played, goals, assists, points and have collected over 1,600 penalty minutes. You'll find Gordie's name in the NHL record book with league marks for the most NHL seasons (26), most 20-goal seasons (22) and for goals (801), assists (1,049) and points (1,850) by a right-winger. He was the first NHL player to reach the 600, 700 and 800-goal plateaus and the first to register 1,000 points and skate in 1,000 games. He retired from the NHL in 1980 as the league's all-time leader in regular-season and playoff scoring.

In his 23rd season as a Red Wings player, at the age of 41, Howe became the first Detroit player to garner a 100-point season, collecting 103 points.

Howe, Frank Mahovlich and Alex Delvecchio combined for 118 goals, an NHL record for linemates.

Gordie retired in 1971 and was looking forward to a career as a Red Wings' executive, but was shunted aside from the spotlight by owner Bruce Norris. It was the way he ended up his career in Detroit that led him to joining the Houston Aeros of the World Hockey Association, but what a mark that allowed him to make on the game. To have accomplished such an unprecedented NHL career, then to go to the WHA at the age of 43 and play with his kids Mark and Marty, just showed how he could play hockey. He won the MVP award in 1973-74, his first season back in big-league hockey after a two-year absence and was a two-time WHA All-Star, winning two Avco Cup championships with the Aeros.

After the 1979 NHL-WHA merger, Gordie came back to the NHL and played alongside Mark and Marty with the Hartford Whalers. When they played in Detroit during the 1979-80 season, Gordie was the first star of Hartford's 6-4 victory on Jan. 12, 1980, and took the opening face-off between his sons when the Whalers and Wings tied 4-4 on March 13. Gordie scored 15 goals that season, which was amazing considering he was the oldest player in NHL history at the age of 52 when the season ended. But the moment everyone will remember fondly that season was when he came back to Detroit for the NHL All-Star Game at the Joe Louis Arena, one of the first big events here. It was just a never-ending standing ovation when he was on the ice, and you could see Gordie's eyes tearing up.

To this day, the adulation for the man they call Mr. Hockey has only grown, but Gordie has never changed, and I think that is one of the attributes of a hockey player. If you look at some of the veterans of the game, like Jean Beliveau and Milt Schmidt, the guys that kept hockey so alive, they never change. They're still about class. They respect their elders and provide good images for other people. I think every team in the Original Six days had two or three players like that who were just a credit to the game. But there's no doubt that of all the great ones who have graced this game, Gordie Howe was the greatest.

They just don't make them like him anymore.

Other Voices

❝ *The arenas when we had six teams, it was so different in many ways, but I was fortunate to be a part of that.*❞

- Budd Lynch

I got into broadcasting hockey at a very fascinating time in the game's history, shortly after World War II had concluded. Several prominent National Hockey League players enlisted in the armed forces to aid the war effort and some of the players were coming back from the war. Montreal defenseman Kenny Reardon, I'd met him overseas. Sid Abel came back to the Red Wings from the Royal Canadian Air Force, and Boston got Frank Brimsek back from the United States Navy.

Going to Boston, going to Chicago, going to New York, I never thought I'd ever be the one on the microphone broadcasting the NHL. I liked sports and did a lot of shows. And I met a lot of characters over the years. The men behind the voice, I guess you could say. And what characters they were.

The six team days of the NHL helped foster some real rivalries within the cities. Naturally, Toronto-Montreal was heated, but so were Detroit-Montreal and Detroit-Toronto. The rivalry between Canada and the U.S. in hockey, I think that helped to build pro hockey. Hockey had been played in Michigan for years. Jack Adams had played in Houghton years before he came to Detroit. Hockey became part of Michigan, no doubt about that. Radio, I think, was a great advertising billboard for selling a sport. And hockey was no exception to that rule.

People don't realize that the Original Six teams, especially the American arenas - Boston, Detroit, New York and Chicago - they were built specifically for boxing and wrestling. They were the two big sports in the 1920s and 1930s. When hockey was getting its explosion, they put in the 200x85 foot rink and the fans are looking down and it got to be the utopia for viewing a hockey game.

At the Olympia in those early days and in most of the arenas, they had chicken wire behind the nets, so the fans could hear the players and the players could hear the reaction of the fans. And they could also hear the voice of the referee. Many a night, certainly they could hear Red Storey yelling, "Look out, he's coming." The defenseman would be going back to get the puck and here's Storey yelling, "He's coming." For a referee to be yelling that, it was unheard of. And some of the foul language you had between players on the ice and on the benches, it could be heard clearly in the seats. NHL president Clarence Campbell was always notifying teams to watch their language.

The arenas when we had six teams, each was so different in many ways, but I was fortunate to be a part of that. The six cities because of the schedule that we played - seven times in each city, seven times against each team at Olympia - it was naturally structured to create intense rivalries. We traveled by train and bus once in a while. The train rides, particularly into Montreal, got to be a thrill. You were part of the family. Detroit general manager Jack Adams insisted that the writers, photographers and broadcasters be a part of the team on a road trip. Whoever heard of that? Adams said, "You can hang around with the players for a while after the game." The Red Wings had a car called RW1 and that was their sleeper.

When you're traveling with a team, and especially with the rookies, I think the Red Wings, perhaps, have done a better job than most people realize in acclimatizing the new players. On the road, the veterans take the rookies with them. That way, it makes the kids feel like they belong. The first time they go to a big city, their eyes are banjo size. The veterans help them out and then eventually, when they get a handle on the place, the

A lineup of legends. Toe Blake, myself, 1937-38 NHL scoring champ Gordie Drillon of Toronto, Foster Hewitt and former Montreal and Toronto star Murph Chamberlain.

younger guys will go their own way.

Broadcasting locations were always a crazy thing, too. When I went to Montreal for the first time, nobody had briefed me on where I was going to work. Well, in Montreal at the Forum, they had this little ledge that hung out and looked down on the visitor's players' bench. The Canadiens were across the way in those days and the penalty box was on their side of the ice. Boston did the same thing and the advantage they had was unfair. That was changed in later years in both rinks.

Doug Smith was the original broadcaster with the Montreal Canadiens in English, and Rene Lecavalier handled the French broadcasts. Then when Danny Gallivan came on the scene from New Brunswick in 1952, replacing Smith -- who'd opted to go exclusively to football broadcasting -- he worked hard. He became the voice of the Canadiens, just as Foster Hewitt became the voice of the Maple Leafs, of course. Danny broadcasted Canadiens' games for 32 years on "Hockey Night In Canada", doing more than 1,800 Montreal games and coining some phrases that became symbolic of his coverage. Montreal won 16 Stanley Cups while he was doing its play-by-play. Imagine that. No other team in NHL history has won more than 11 Cups. He even played himself in a 1975 movie, "The Million Dollar Hockey Puck", during which he broadcasted the play-by-play of a Canadiens-Red Wings game. His broadcast booth was right beside us, and Bruce Martyn and I, we'd be on the air and we'd say, "We're going to be joined by Foster Hewitt's standby, Danny Gallivan of the Montreal Canadiens." Well, Danny would lean out and say, "Welcome to the Montreal Forum, home of the Montreal Canadiens, defending Stanley Cup champions," and he'd go on and on. He had this cardboard sheet, like the ones you get in the back of a shirt from the dry cleaners, and he had all of those phrases he used - cannonading, exhilarating, enormous -- he had all of them written on the sheet. The action hadn't even started yet and he'd be throwing them into the broadcast already. He was a good kid, Danny. He got sick too soon and we lost him to heart failure at such a young age in 1993. He was only 75 at the time of his death.

We had that infamous riot in Montreal, the "Rocket Richard riot" – a travesty on hockey -- and as Montreal GM Frank Selke once said, "it was a blight that should have never happened." Clarence Campbell, the president of the National Hockey League, a good personal friend of mine because I knew him overseas -- he was a Rhodes Scholar and he was involved with the war crimes trials following World War II -- he ruled with a firm hand in many ways and a lot of it never got out in print. He fined Lefty Wilson one time for yelling at the officials, and poor Lefty didn't know what to do. "Five hundred dollars?" he said, but Adams paid it for him.

When the Rocket lost his temper in a game at Boston – he took after one of the players and used not his stick, but another player's stick to go after him -- harsh action had to be taken. And then in the hotel the next morning, before they caught the train to go back to Montreal, he accosted the linesman again, making matters worse. Clarence Campbell got the report from the referee, and as the Canadiens were on their way back to Montreal, he made the announcement -- suspended for the rest of the season and the playoffs. Here is the image of hockey in Montreal and French-Canadians from coast-to-coast and he's out for the season.

Detroit played in Montreal on March 17, 1955, the day after Campbell made his announcement of Rocket's suspension. The Arena in Montreal seated about 15,000 people, and they warned Clarence not to come to the game. He had seats that he paid for in the building every year, and he had his secretary with him, later his wife. In the first period, Earl Reibel and Red Kelly each scored twice and the Wings were ahead 4-1. Being in the army, I noticed the smell of tear gas right away. And then smoke started filling the building. There was a scuffle over by where Clarence was sitting and someone accosted him. Jimmy Orlando, the tough old Red Wings defenseman who lived in Montreal, he came up and decked the guy and he went down right away, falling down the aisle. Finally, the French-Canadian engineer turned to my broadcast partner Al Nagler and I, and said, "The game is being forfeited. We've got two policemen here to take you to the (Detroit) dressing room." We packed up and we were escorted down to the room. They tried to empty the building and it took them a long time to do that. We got in the dressing room and Jack Adams said that Frank Selke had put a note under the door saying, "Regretfully, the game is forfeited. So you win 1-0." We were escorted to our bus to take us to Westmount Station, where the train came in from New York. But we were up there two hours early. And then the conductor at the railway station, he was keeping us posted, telling Jack what was happening.

It was a riot. They had 25,000 people in the streets. They poured in from the suburbs. They damaged buildings, turned over streetcars, turned over police cars, broke windows. Total cost of the repairs was pegged in the hundreds of thousands of dollars. The damage was done and it was a blight on the career of the Rocket.

It's too bad, because that Rocket Richard, what a competitor he was. Every team had an outstanding player in the six-team era during the 1950s. Toronto had Teeder Kennedy, Boston had Milt Schmidt and later in the decade, Chicago got Bobby Hull and New York added Andy Bathgate, all of them great players.

Having grown up in Hamilton, Ontario, so close to Toronto, I think the Maple Leafs with Foster Hewitt were on every station. They had Wes McKnight on before the game and during the intermission; they had the Beehive Golden Corn Syrup photos that you could send away for. That was an era when Toronto and Montreal really marketed hockey in Canada.

The recognition that honors all of us broadcasters when we are enshrined in the Hockey Hall of Fame is known as the Foster Hewitt Award because he was the father of hockey play-by-play. I worked with Foster at the gondola at the famed Maple Leaf Gardens for many years. When I first broadcasted there, I'll tell you, it was quite an experience. I'd heard about the gondola, but nothing could accurately describe the experience of going up there for the first time. You walked up to the grays, then got on a catwalk, which was a swaying bridge, and you walked over the people's heads below to the gondola, which was hung right over the ice.

I remember the first time Bruce Martyn walked out there with me; Bruce got sick. Some of the Hollywood stars who'd be in town filming movies, they'd want to see the gondola, but many of them were too afraid to go out there. Others would crawl on their hands and knees.

I met Foster overseas as well when he was entertaining the troops. He was not a big man, but he was a dapper little guy. He used to always say, "I wish I was seven-feet tall because I have trouble looking in people's eyes." He told me one time, jokingly, "You've got to invest." And I'd say, "Well, you've got to have money to invest. I'm just trying to get by on what I've got. After all, I've got a family, you know." He'd say, "You've got to buy General

Motors stock." I'd answer, "Yeah, General Motors." I guess that's where he'd made his original fortune, when General Motors was first starting out.

Foster used to love to go for Chinese food, so we'd always go to Victor Lim's in downtown Detroit by the city hall. He ate there so much that Victor and his wife made up a special dish, Hawaiian Shrimp on a stick, and called it "He Shoots and He Gets It." Foster would always insist that I'd have dinner two or three times a year with him in Toronto and we'd go to the Royal York Hotel. They had a big band there.

Foster Hewitt asked me to do a favor one time. He knew that somebody in Toronto was stealing his broadcasting coverage. Our coverage was carried as far as London and sometimes repeated in Hamilton. So he said in the third period only, add five seconds to every penalty call. So if it was at 3:14, I'd say 3:19. When a goal is scored, add five seconds. So I added the five seconds. Foster called me a couple of days later. He said he'd caught the guy. Joe Crysdale was the broadcaster. They were listening in and repeating the broadcast on the air. Foster said, "I had to nail somebody."

Bill Hewitt, Foster's son, ultimately took over the Leafs' broadcasts from his dad in 1961 and was the voice of the Leafs on "Hockey Night in Canada" for two decades. I think Billy really wanted to become a great broadcaster, but Foster overshadowed the kid in so many ways. Foster would bring Billy on during "Young Canada Night" at Maple Leaf Gardens every year to broadcast a portion of the game from the time Billy was eight years old. They worked together on the broadcasts from 1955 until Foster switched exclusively to radio in 1961. Billy actually had a bodyguard, a big, former cop form London, England, but a nice guy. Foster called one time and said, "Billy's coming up with him to do the game. Help him out as best you can." When they got there, I told them I'd have a guy available if they wanted anything. At the end of the game, Detroit won and I said to Billy, "Come on, I'll take you guys and we'll go to Lindell AC." The train didn't go until 2:30 in the morning. So he gets his briefcase and he gives it to owner Jimmy Butsicaris to put behind the bar. He has a couple of beers and Jimmy was all excited to see Foster's son there, so he stands up and says, "Billy Hewitt, Foster's pride and joy, wants to buy the entire bar a drink." Billy got a little upset and he disappeared. He and the bodyguard went and got a cab, but they left the briefcase behind. I said to Jimmy, "I've got an idea." We got his car and we drove to the depot. I phoned the porter, a guy I knew from the many trips we'd made, and I said, "I've got a favor to ask you. You've got Billy Hewitt, Foster's son, on board and here's his briefcase. He left it downtown. Now when you get to Chatham, Ontario, knock on his berth and tell him his briefcase is on board. I'm sure he'll appreciate it and I'll give you a $20 bill for looking after it." I ripped the bill in two and gave him half. "The other half will be at the Lindell when you come back," I told him. So he did. After Chatham, he knocked on the door and told Bill the briefcase was on board. Later, Foster told me, "You sure took care of Billy. How much did it cost Jimmy Butsicaris to buy the whole bar a drink?" I took Foster down there one time to try and meet the guy, the porter who'd returned Billy's briefcase.

Poor Billy couldn't handle alcohol for one thing. He was a loner and always wanted to be a fly-boy. He took the entire "Hockey Night in Canada" crew up in a plane one time. Billy landed the plane perfectly and they showed it during the intermission. It was a cute clip that they had, but Foster called Billy the next day and told him, "You are not flying anymore. You are not buying that plane. You are not flying in a plane at all unless it's a commercial flight." Well, he was the only kid, the heir apparent, so I guess Foster wanted to be sure he didn't lose him. Foster had a terrific radio station, CKFH -- the 'FH' standing for Foster Hewitt. And I guess they had a beautiful resort area home in Huntsville, Ontario, in the Muskoka Lakes area.

The last days of Olympia. Joining Elliot Trumbull. Gordie Howe. Art Skov. Alex Delvecchio. Marcel Pronovost. Jimmy Peters. Billy Dea and Johnny Wilson to say good-bye to our longtime home shortly before it met the wrecking ball.

Billy, later on, his first wife divorced him and he remarried. He went into a shell and never showed again at the Gardens or at any hockey events for that matter. He died in 1996.

You can't talk about the Leafs without talking about legendary owner Harold Ballard. In junior hockey, with the Marlies, he and Windsor's Jimmy Skinner, who later coached the Red Wings to the Stanley Cup in 1954-55, they had some pretty good feuds.

After Detroit-Toronto games at Maple Leaf Gardens, Ballard would always see me on the way out and say, "You've got to come have dinner with us." And I'd say, "No, I'm on my way home. I don't eat at this hour." "Well, you've got to come and sit with my friend then." He had some characters he hung around with. So I'd go over and he'd start out by saying, "This is a young Canadian officer who became a turncoat and went to the States to make money with those damn Red Wings." That's the way he introduced me all of the time.

I think Ballard pulled the greatest trick ever. The Rochester Americans were the American Hockey League farm club of the Maple Leafs. The American Bowling Congress tournament was coming into Rochester one year and wanted to put the lanes in the arena. So Ballard talked the people in Rochester into okaying the idea and moved some Rochester games to Toronto. In May, he sent all of the season-ticket holders at Maple Leaf Gardens a release stating that by the end of May, "You will renew your season tickets and you also have 12 junior Toronto Marlboro tickets and 14 Rochester Americans tickets." He had all that money in the till in May and he made sure those Rochester seats would be sold.

Another legendary Maple Leafs player, coach and executive was King Clancy. Clancy was one of those great characters you meet in a lifetime. He and Jack Adams had played hockey together in the NHL with the Ottawa Senators. They won a Stanley Cup together as teammates in Ottawa in 1926-27. I'd heard stories that they'd also played together in Houghton, Michigan.

I think Clancy was perhaps the fall guy for everything in Toronto. Nobody would ever dare criticize the King. Francis, that was his given name, a good Irishman and he was a great character, loved by everyone. Jack Adams gave him a thrill at Olympia one time. St. Patrick's Day was coming up on the 17th of March. We had a home game against Toronto, and Jack had the ice painted green. The league objected to that, so did the referee, but it was too late. The ice was painted a colorful green.

Our broadcasting locations varied from rink to rink. At the old Madison Square Garden in New York, there were fans all around you. Foster Hewitt had tipped me off. He said, "At the Garden, be careful. The (MSG) president's wife sits up there and she'll be throwing beer and bottle caps at you." She hated the visitors. Later on, she became a member of Alcoholics Anonymous, and she'd entertain the hockey players who were having trouble. But that's how vicious she was at one time. You got a paper cup full of beer from her every game.

I remember they had these old guys in New York. They looked about 74 or 75 years old, and they'd be out there scraping the ice between periods in the days before the Zamboni. It was really something to see.

At Chicago Stadium, we counted 998 steps to get to our location for radio. When I switched to television, the distance was only about half of that. Radio was way up and they sold beer at every level. We were up on the same level as the organist, Al Melgard, who was a great organist. He only had nine fingers, but boy he could rap those keys. When the officials would come on the ice, he'd play three blind mice. He got fined for it, too. The vibration of the organ, you could see your microphone moving on the desk.

Chicago Stadium was an exciting place to work, but what a tough neighborhood. They had a dog, a big dog in a wire cage outside the rink. One night, a pane of glass broke behind the goalie at one end. They held the game up. The referee, Frank Udvari, and the linesmen were checking things out. I'm trying to describe the scene and then a couple of the rink attendants came up with part of the dog cage and were lashing that together to make for some protection back there. But I kept wondering, "Where's the dog?" They said, "Don't worry, Budd, he's down by the visitor's dressing room."

The Chicago fans, they'd get there about 4 o'clock, 4:30 when the doors opened, and the game didn't start until 7:30. They'd get up there in the first two rows of the balcony with their decks of cards and they'd play cards. In the third period, if the game wasn't going their way, they'd take a deck of cards, put an elastic band around it, and throw them on the ice. The officials would be left to play 52 pick-up. It was unbelievable how long that would hold the game up.

Boston Garden was another great place to work. You were in a hanger out over the ice. The crowd was wild there. Those Bostonians, they knew their hockey. In those days, they had the penalty box right next to the Boston Bruins bench. They had an organ there that was actually only eight rows up above the ice surface. I guess the guy was afraid of heights, but boy, he'd get that crowd flying, just like the organist in Chicago. The fans that would come there, the Gallery Gods they would call them. I always said of the Boston Garden that every year they'd put another layer of paint on it and pretend like they had a brand new building. Boston Garden was always painted mustard. The Jacobs brothers from Buffalo , New York, who owned the team, were big, big operators of concessions for stadiums and they painted it mustard to make people think of wanting to buy hot dogs, I guess.

A lot of people didn't realize that we had an organ at the Olympia at the one end where the Zamboni came out. That's where the visiting broadcasters had to work. Foster Hewitt used to work there. And the organist used to like to nip. There'd be 10 empty mickeys underneath the stands because nobody ever cleaned the place.

When expansion first came to the NHL starting in 1967, there were certain cities that had minor-league hockey like Buffalo. Buffalo had some great American Hockey League teams through the years, and because it was so close to the border, it was an international crowd. Expansion made our jobs a lot tougher, though. There were many more players that we now had to know. My theory was, as a broadcaster, we're going to have to get a program to figure out who's playing for whom.

Today, they've got 30 teams to deal with in places like Tampa Bay and Nashville and Anaheim and approximately 650 names of players to keep track of during the season. I don't know how the guys do it.

My Brother And I

CHAPTER NINE

❝ *I had no brother and he had no brother, but we are brothers.*"

- Bruce Martyn

They say that everyone has a twin somewhere in the world. I don't know about that, but when I was first paired in the broadcast booth with Bruce Martyn in 1964, I soon discovered that I had a brother.

Bruce used to have a saying – I had no brother and he had no brother, but we are brothers. It was so true. I don't think two fellows could have gotten along better. I don't believe that we ever had a disagreement.

The first time I met Bruce, though, it was a funny story, although Bruce certainly wasn't laughing much at the time. Fred Huber was the public relations director for the hockey club and the night the Red Wings were going to play the Soo Greyhounds in an exhibition game during training camp, Bruce, who worked in Sault Ste. Marie at the time, was going to do the broadcast. Bruce said, "Oh I hope they're listening in Detroit. I'm sure they're waiting to hear me. I've been doing hockey up here for years. Somebody's got to want me down there." And I said, "Don't worry, they'll hear you."

Bruce worked so hard at it and when Fred Huber got through the introductions at ice level and pointed to Bruce, and said, "You're on," Bruce picked up the mic and said, "Good evening hockey fans and welcome to Tiger Stadium." He had listened to so much baseball over the years, I guess it was in the back of his mind.

I spent 12 great years working with Bruce, who finally joined me in the booth after working on both Detroit Lions and Michigan State football before making the switch to hockey and the Red Wings. Coming into the booth in the mid-1960s, he was with the team when it was up and down like a yo-yo, calling the games while suffering through a lot of lean years for the hockey club. He called two Stanley Cup finals involving the Red Wings – in 1966 and 1995, but Detroit lost both of them, first to the Montreal Canadiens and then to the New Jersey Devils. Bruce retired after that 1995 final without ever knowing my thrill of calling a winning Detroit Stanley Cup goal, so that's why it was so wonderful of Ken Kal, who followed Bruce as the team's radio play-by-play voice, to bring Bruce back and let him do one period of that Stanley Cup game. It also shows you what a class act Ken Kal is as both a broadcaster and a human being.

As it turned out, Bruce called the second period and that's when Darren McCarty scored what turned out to be the Stanley Cup-winning goal for the Red Wings, the first one by the team since I called Gordie Howe's Cup winner against the Canadiens back in 1955. I was so happy for Bruce that he finally got to feel that thrill. And Ken's known the same excited feeling twice since then, when Detroit won the Cup in 1998 and again in 2002, which goes to show you that there is something to this karma business. Do something nice for someone and you will be rewarded handsomely in kind.

Bruce and I worked both radio and television broadcasts during our time together in the booth. We had some great times together and we really hit it off, right from the beginning. In fact, the only difficulties we ever had seemed to center around our glasses.

Back in those days, we'd use the intermission breaks to switch back-and-forth between the booths. I'd do two periods on radio and then go and do the third period on TV. In certain cities, you had long distances between the radio booth and the TV location. In Boston Garden this one time, Bruce had been doing two periods of radio, and I had done two periods of TV. I'm coming over to relieve him. He gets up and I'm chewing the fat with a guest. Bruce is standing there and he should be over to the TV booth by now because they're getting ready to drop the puck. Finally, I said, "What's wrong?" and he said, "I can't find my glasses." I used my glasses for reading scripts, but Bruce, he needed his to see the length and the width of the ice. We started laughing, but he didn't see what was so funny, until I pointed to his shirt. They were sticking out of his pocket. He forgot he'd put them back in their case.

Another time, in our rush to get from one end of the rink to the other, we grabbed each other's glasses. Well, I'm far-sighted and he's near-sighted, so I couldn't read and he couldn't see for about a period until somebody ran down and changed our glasses. That's the sort of mayhem that happened when we worked side by side.

Poor Bruce. When we traveled when Pit Martin was on the team, especially when the team was in Montreal, of all places, Bruce would have four calls waiting for him, all in French and all for Pit. The joys of traveling. Some people, it really bothers them. Bruce, he couldn't stand traveling. Me, I kept myself occupied, every place I ever went. I had friends in Montreal because I'd worked there after the war. I had friends in a lot of cities. The Gleason family in Boston, they had seats behind the Bruins' bench, but they were big Red Wings' fans and good friends with Sid Abel. They'd entertain us once in a while with dinner at their house. They'd make us these 8-10 pound lobsters that were just delicious.

We'd have a fine dinner and afterwards, Sid, Alex Delvecchio, Lefty Wilson, and myself, we'd go sit on the porch and smoke. Mrs. Gleason was very proud of her home, so we never smoked in her house.

As I told Bruce one time, I guess as a kid traveling so much -- I traveled my whole life -- I find there's something about every city that you don't know.

"Don't stay in the hotel on the road," I'd tell Bruce. Some players, some broadcasters and writers, they get glued to their room. They just don't want to get out. I've had some great experiences by simply going out that hotel door.

One time in New York, I went down to the waterfront to see the big ships, the liners. It's quite a sight to see. I went to this little pub down by the waterfront and there was this chap standing there and he said to me, "Where you from?" So I told him, and he said, "What do you do?" I told him I worked for the Detroit Red Wings. "We have a game here tomorrow night, so I'm killing time here." So then he said, "What do you know about water?" I told him my dad had worked for Canada Steamship Lines and when I was a kid I'd worked on a boat. Then he said, "I'm the captain of a tugboat, would you like to go out on a tug the next time you're here?" I was flattered. "We take the garbage out to the Atlantic," he said. I looked at the schedule and I told him, "I'll be back here in a couple of weeks time." He said, "When you hit town the next time, you call me here at my home number and if it's possible, you'll come on the boat as my guest."

Next time in, I called and he's been waiting for me. "Yep, we're going out," he says. His boat is a tug towing these four great big garbage scows, each of them the size of an arena. We're going at a snail's pace, there were only five people on board and one of them is a chef. With the weight of all that garbage, the tug is bouncing all over the place on the water. Well, I'd never been seasick in my life, not even during the war going into France on D-Day, and I wasn't going to be this time, either. Anyway, we get out so far, they make their turn and they had a way of discharging all of that crap into the ocean. I don't imagine they do it that way anymore, what with all the concern today about the environment. Now we're heading back, about a three-hour trip, and the chef puts on a meal of steaks, hot rolls and buttered corn. What a way to recover from dumping garbage. I got them tickets for the next hockey game.

Little crazy things like that always seem to come from getting out of the room and discovering the place where I was visiting. I think by traveling, the joys of traveling have their shortcomings at times, but you just have to make the best of the situation. Being associated with the hockey team definitely had its benefits because you were welcome at so many places and you met so many people. I remember this one time, Jack Berry was one of the writers covering a trip with us to Boston. Jack's dad had been a traveling secretary with the Detroit Tigers, and Jack wore his dad's World Series ring.

He said to me, "Where's your Stanley Cup ring?" And I said, "The only one I've got, my daughter wears." We're killing time in Boston and I say, "This is such a beautiful city and I love coming here, let's get a cab and see the sites. So we go down to the waterfront, we see Old Ironsides, then we go down to where all the restaurants are on the wharf. We ate at Jimmy's Harborside, which was owned by a guy who was from Detroit. On the waterfront, they had the mothball fleet, the carriers from World War II. And then you'd see the lobster fleet coming in. I could tell I had piqued Jack's interest with my impromptu tour. After dinner, he said, "Where we going now?" And I said, "You're a Catholic, I'm a Catholic, I'm going to take you somewhere I've always wanted to see. A friend of mine is going to meet us there." Barry Baker was the fellow, and he took us to Eddie's church in Boston. There was this guy there and he took us in and showed us around. Berry said, "How do we get out?" I said, "The same way as we came in.

There's only one door."

On another occasion, I took Bruce to an Italian restaurant in Chicago. There's some great restaurants in that city. We get there and the place is jammed, but I know there's a backroom. Well, the owner sees me and brings Bruce and I back there to a table. He brings a bottle of wine out and then a cigar. The owner loved cigars. We had a bite to eat and the owner says, "Your timing is great, Budd. It's our last night. They're tearing the place down to put in a parking lot tomorrow." There was so many of these little Italian bistros in Chicago, I guess it was a hard time making a go of it.

For all the years I spent calling games, luckily, I never had laryngitis. I never lost my voice and never missed a broadcast. Bruce wasn't so fortunate.

One time, I had to give him my secret recipe. When your voice is tired, especially after those long overtime games, you hear that strain in your voice. We had one of those games one time in Chicago and you could hear the impact it had made on Bruce's vocal chords. So after the game, I told Bruce my theory. "OK what?" he said. After the game, we went to the bar, and I ordered us two hot buttered rums with a cinnamon stick in each of them. "Now Bruce, we're going to our rooms," I told him. So we carry our drinks upstairs. I tell him to go into the bathroom and put the steamer on. Then strip and put a towel over your head like a boxer and sip that hot buttered rum. Now you're finishing your drink, your body is loosening up and your pours are opening up. Now get into bed and get four hours of solid sleep and then call me in the morning. For some reason, it works.

That was one of the many tricks of the trade I learned from the greats over the years. Mel Allen used to carry codeine with him all the time, and he was the one who told me about the hot buttered rum.

I retired from broadcasting in 1975, and 20 years later, Bruce, who switched exclusively to radio in 1986, hung up his microphone. But in

On opening night of the 1991-92 season, the 75th anniversary of the NHL, Bruce Martyn and I welcomed Stu Evans, at the time the oldest living Red Wing.

between, history reunited us one last time and it was a humdinger. Not a great game, mind you, but definitely the most unbelievable tale involving Bruce and I in the booth.

The classic one with Bruce and I was in 1991-92, when the NHL was celebrating its 75th year. Every city in the Original Six decided to do something different and the team asked me, "Would you mind doing a period of a game in Toronto with Bruce?" Bruce and I talked about it and we both thought, "Yeah, that's a good idea." So we went to Maple Leaf Gardens.

Toronto was ahead 5-1. In those days, you didn't have the mouthpiece and headset, you had the metal stand microphone. Bruce turns it over to me to start the third period and says, "Toronto 5, Detroit 1. Hold the lead, Budd." That was his introduction. Toronto had it all over the Wings that night. The game got out of hand and I think it ended up 6-4. But in the third period, for some reason, in my moving around with one wing, I just happened to knock the mic out of the stand. Bruce described the thing on-air to the listeners. And can you picture this? Here's the one-armed guy, reeling the cord in, hoping the mic doesn't fall off the cord and plummet into the fans below, bringing it up so far and then locking it between my knees, fishing with one arm and Bruce is laughing into the other mic. I'm going through the same thing. I don't want the mic to fall and hit somebody. I finally get it up and put it back in the stand, and the poor engineer had left the mic on, so did that ever hurt Bruce's ears. I said, "The next time, maybe WJR will spend a little more money and put headsets on us." Bruce tried to describe the whole scene and he said to me, "It's a good thing you didn't lose a leg or you would have never been able to get that mic back."

When Bruce went into the Hall of Fame in 1991, I got a hold of Danny Gallivan because we were all such good friends. Danny was a loner, he didn't mingle too much, but he and I got along well. Bruce went into the Hall of Fame after 30 years with the Red Wings. Danny didn't drink, but he'd always hold on to a glass. He was cute. I had a picture taken in Toronto with the three of us together and it's one of my cherished mementos.

I still see Bruce and his wife Donna all the time. They're enjoying retirement in Venice, Florida, and I make it a point to visit them whenever possible. After all, he is my brother.

Lean Years

CHAPTER TEN

" *After the gathering comes the scattering."*
- Irish Proverb

I started broadcasting Red Wings games during the 1949-50 NHL season, and the team celebrated four Stanley Cup triumphs during my first six years at the mic. That was an era when the Wings were a competitive, well-organized and well-balanced team, one of three dominant powers in the NHL from the early 1940s through the late 1960s. In the time frame between 1942-69, Detroit, the Montreal Canadiens and the Toronto Maple Leafs won every Stanley Cup title except for one. Montreal was a great champion in the second half of the 1950s and into the 1960s and beyond, and Toronto came along, too, as a regular contender in the late 1950s.

After the 1954-55 season, which was the fourth Cup title I'd called as Detroit's play-by-play voice, the Wings continued to contend for the next decade, but could never seem to clear that final hurdle.

Poor Bruce Martyn. He worked with me for 12 years and he suffered, because for so many years, he went through the trial and error where they'd get so far, get into the playoffs and get knocked off. His whole career, we often talked about it, he proved he was a jinx. Even when the team went to the finals, they'd get knocked off.

Montreal ended Detroit's record seven-season run as a first-place club in 1956-57 and also whipped the Wings four straight in the Stanley Cup final. It was the beginning of a string of heartbreaking trips to the final for the club. The Wings would reach the pinnacle of the playoffs four more times between 1961-66, but victory was never theirs to celebrate.

In 1961, Chicago downed Detroit in six games to win the Stanley Cup, the first victory by the Black Hawks since 1938. Two years later, Toronto whipped Detroit in a five-game final series. The same two teams met the following spring in a thrilling seven-game set.

That was the year that Toronto defenseman Bobby Baun got hit late in Game 6 with a Gordie Howe shot and was stretchered off the ice. He was in the dressing room with a broken bone in his ankle, but then he comes out in the overtime and wins the game. It just shows you that injuries are injuries, but some players have the knack to play over them. In the early days, you would never admit you were injured because you didn't want to go to the minors. The Wings were up 3-2 in the series at that point, playing on home ice with a 3-2 lead, when Toronto's Billy Harris tied the game at 17:48 of the third period. Think about that. Detroit was 2:12 away from winning the Stanley Cup. Then Harris scores and Baun wins it with a shot from the point at 2:43 of overtime. Baun played another 35 playoff games the remainder of his NHL career, including four with Detroit in 1970, and never scored another goal. No wonder the Wings were so shell-shocked they were blanked 4-0 at Toronto in Game 7.

Overtime goals can be heartbreakers, and that was the case when Detroit lost the 1966 final to Montreal on a goal that Detroit players of that season still claim should have been disallowed.

The Wings won the first two games of that series at Montreal, then lost three straight, but sent Game 6 at Olympia to overtime tied 2-2 when Floyd Smith scored with 9:30 left in regulation. Early in the first overtime session, Montreal's Henri Richard went down on the ice at the Grand River end, got tangled up with Detroit defenseman Gary Bergman, and they both fell to the ice. I can still see Richard's glove on the puck. The next thing I knew, the referee blew the whistle. The puck's in, the light's on. I remember the referee going back to ask the goal judge how it went in and the goal judge just shook his head and said he hadn't seen it. A lot of the players, even to today, insist that goal should have never counted. The puck was along the ice, going toward the net and with his arm, his glove, Richard steered that puck into the net, there's no doubt about it. Too bad they didn't have replay in those days. That's one time when it certainly would have come in handy.

The Canadiens were so excited about it, they never came out on the ice to congratulate the Wings on the series. They went straight to the dressing room. The referee, Frank Udvari, said, "Well, the goal judge saw the puck when he put the light on." You felt sorry in a sense for goal judges, because sometimes their power of concentration would really be tested. Under NHL rules, they're supposed to be in a cage, but in Montreal for years, the goal judge was right in the middle of the fans. They wouldn't put a cage around him and as a result, their concentration suffered.

Detroit Roger Crozier played so well in that playoff, he won the Conn Smythe Trophy as Stanley Cup MVP even though he'd been on the losing side, the first that had ever happened.

The Wings have always been fortunate to have good goaltending, starting with the Lumley-Sawchuk years, and Crozier followed splendidly. He was voted rookie of the year in 1964-65, and that season he became the last goaltender in NHL history to appear in all of his team's games, making

70 starts.

Crozier had a stomach problem. He couldn't eat spicy foods. When the team would go to Montreal, in particular, they'd always go to the deli across the street from the hotel and bring in pastrami and all the nice food they could get. Poor Roger couldn't eat any of it, so he was the waiter.

They called him Roger the dodger. What a wiry goaltender he was, but so acrobatic. He was so small, he made sure he was between those pipes all the time. He had a favorite trick of his. Periodically, he'd take his goal stick and hang it on the crossbar and swing from it like a parrot in a cage. He was a very playful guy. During his days with Buffalo, he was great there, too, helping the Sabres to their first Stanley Cup final in 1974-75.

Goalies are such a unique breed. They're loners most of the time. Some of them get moved so fast to other teams, the people don't understand how they started. Roger came up in the Chicago system, but with Glenn Hall in front of him, he caught a break when he was traded to Detroit. Some of these goalies can really skate. Eddie Giacomin of the New York Rangers, who finished his career with Detroit in the late 1970s, was a good skater, and he was one of the first ones to go behind the net and actually stickhandle back there and defy somebody to take the puck away from him.

Although Detroit's run of Stanley Cups may have halted in the 1950s, the Wings fans were still blessed to see many great players don the winged wheel, including then-future Hall of Famers like Bill Gadsby. He was a great defensive competitor, and one thing he always used to say about his career was he scored more goals his first year than Gordie Howe did. He was right, too. They both broke into the league in 1946-47. Gadsby scored eight times in 48 games for Chicago, one more than Gordie tallied in 58 games with Detroit. Mr. Hockey got him in the long run, though, outscoring Bill, 801-130, during their respective NHL careers.

Gadsby was nicknamed The Bear, although some of the guys called him Ears due to the way they seemed to protrude from the side of his head. He was an inspiration as a defenseman and he loved to take face-offs. A lot of defensemen loved to take face-offs in those days and the practice was fairly commonplace around the league. During the 1966 playoffs, Sports Illustrated took a picture of Gadsby and Chicago's Stan Mikita in a face-off and they put it on the cover. The puck is dropped by the linesman and Bill's stick is behind Mikita's neck, driving his head down between his legs. He didn't even put the stick on the ice for the face-off.

Mikita and Gadsby were both determined competitors, but they became good friends afterwards, and that's one thing about the sport. The camaraderie among hockey players runs deeper than in any other sport. When Lou Fontinato and Gordie Howe got into that mess one time in New York, the big fight they had in 1961, later on, Lou went out of his way to see Gordie and talk about it, which was really something, because at the time, Fontinato was the policeman in the NHL, the tough guy, but he just messed up when he went after Gordie Howe.

Another defenseman who came up in that era and showed great potential until his career was tragically cut short was Doug Barkley. He was a tough defenseman and a good puck carrier. He could do an awful lot of things on the ice and he was competitive. His 11 goals in 1963-64 led all NHL defenders. He was just coming into his own at that time and accidentally took a shot to the eye at Olympia on Jan. 30, 1966. I think it was Doug Mohns who shot it and it caught Barkley flush in the cheekbone.

The Norris family went out of their way to help him. They sent Barkley to every hospital in the country that had an eye specialist, including the eye institute in Boston. When he was down there this one time, I went to see him in the hospital the night before the Wings were to play the Bruins at Boston Garden, and the doctor said, "I'll give him permission to come to the game." So he sat with me up in the press box with the doctor beside him, just to see hockey again. There was no way they were ever going to get his sight back, and they had to put the glass eye in. But he hung around and he was a guy who could still do things his own way. He was a credit to anybody who loses something, displaying to everyone that there's still life to live.

He lives in Western Canada and was a hunter. Every time we'd go out on the road, he'd buy a gun and Danny Olesevich, the assistant trainer, had to dismantle it and put it in the kit bag so that we could get it back to Detroit, so that Doug could take it out west with him. He worked for the Calgary Flames as a radio game analyst for many years and came to Joe Louis Arena many times. He was always the same, and we've always kept in touch. He's been through a couple of serious illnesses, but he's bounced back from them.

He was a credit to hockey, the way he described games. Sid Abel was the same, very smart and astute when it came to their observations. When players become analysts on broadcasts, some of them are capable of being the backup, but others are given the job and it never works out. Former Bruins great Johnny Bucyk, whose NHL career started in Detroit, is another good example of a successful transition from the ice to the booth. As a player, Bucyk never wanted it to end. He played 23 seasons until finally hanging them up at the age of 42, in 1978. He was out of hockey and his career was over, so they started using him on the Boston broadcasts, and the fans really went for him. When he'd say something, he was doing it from the point of view of what he remembered; it was like going through that situation. And that's the role the ex-athlete has to play as the No. 2 man in the broadcast booth.

As tough as those Stanley Cup final losses were to stomach, there was one factor that continued to pack them in at Olympia and anywhere on the road, no matter where Detroit stood in the standings - the man who wore No. 9 for the Red Wings.

Gordie Howe was in demand in every arena, but he was a Red Wing

This was quite the coup for me. It wasn't easy to get Wings icon Gordie Howe and Montreal legend Maurice (Rocket) Richard this close together without a fiery exchange between the two superstars. This interview was done during a 1961 charity game.

from the day he signed. Jack Adams always preached that when you put on a Red Wings' jersey, you're representing not only Detroit, but parts of Michigan, parts of Ohio, parts of Ontario and even parts of Illinois, because hockey was heard in those areas. Gordie had no free time anyplace he went - a restaurant, the movies - it didn't matter. But he was always a cooperative guy. He did things that made some other hockey players proud when they heard what he's done. When he signed an autograph, he'd always say, "Did you say please?" And after he gave it to them, he'd say, "And now what do you say?" Naturally, the proper response was, "Thank you." He'd always get the kids, the young girls, too, to say "Thank you." Bobby Hull picked up on that and used to do it, too. He'd ask them why they wanted it, and they'd say, "For my brother. Please."

Gordie was rewriting the NHL record book during the 1960s, which was odd, because Gordie was not desirous of setting records. He was just a God-given, naturally talented Canadian boy who just played so well every night, whether he was at home or on the road. The record that really caught the attention of the hockey world came when Gordie began to zero in on the NHL career goals record of 544 held by Montreal's great Rocket Richard. One night, he finally tied the Rocket in a game on the road, in of all places, Montreal. Then he had to beat the Rocket. Everyone was abuzz. The Rocket was going to have his record broken by Gordie Howe of Detroit. Wow! I don't think Gordie had a desire to surpass anyone, but he knew he was on that threshold of one more goal. There were a couple of occasions where Gordie, because of his unselfishness as a player, would pass the puck when he had a chance at a pretty good shot. Gordie was like that. He was not an egomaniac that wanted to set records. But that was the talk of hockey at the time. The record-breaker eventually had to come, but he waited five games to get No. 545. It came Nov. 10, 1963, at Olympia against Montreal, while the Wings were killing a penalty. Marcel Pronovost started the play. He passed to Gordie in the Detroit end and he, in turn, sent the puck over to Billy McNeill. Howe took a return feed from McNeill and fired a low shot past Canadiens goalie Charlie Hodge.

Elliott Trumbull was the P.R. director for Detroit at the time, and he lined up 545 pucks on the ice and took a picture of Gordie with the pucks. I kidded him, "Did you count the pucks?" and he said, "The trainer counted them." It was a cute picture, though.

While there's no doubt they were both superstar players, there was one thing that gave Gordie an edge. The Rocket had a temper and it backfired on him at times. The Rocket was a thrill to watch, though. I got to know him off and on the ice and once, I got a picture taken with him and Gordie together. Everyone said, "How'd you get them together?" And I said, "Well, when they're on the ice playing, you wouldn't talk to them." But I got them together once and the Rocket consented to it and we got the picture of us together.

Individually, there were nights to celebrate, mostly thanks to Gordie, but even his greatness couldn't prevent the aroma of all things Red Wing from becoming an extremely unpleasant scent. When Bruce Martyn worked with me for the first 12 years, we never really had a great year. From the 1966-67 season through the 1976-77 campaign, the Wings failed to win a single playoff game. In fact, they made the playoffs just once, during the 1969-70 season and were promptly swept by Chicago in four consecutive games. They called that series the spring of 4-2, because all four games ended up 4-2 in favor of the Blackhawks.

I think the decline in fortunes started simply because the club had set the standard so high; other teams were gunning for the Red Wings in that era. It's like when the New York Yankees were great in baseball, everyone wanted to get to them. With the money the Yankees had to spend, they had a team every year that was capable of winning everything. But the other teams, they were catching up and they'd get better hitting and better pitching ,and I think that's what happened to the Red Wings, especially with expansion.

There was a tapering off period in the talent pool with expansion and now there were other teams going for the Stanley Cup. Who ever thought a team like Tampa Bay would win the Stanley Cup? I guess it shows if you've got a good organization, good talent and the breaks of the game, you can make it happen. A lot of teams suffer key injuries at the wrong time or they would have been champions, too.

The Wings missed the playoffs in 1970-71, Gordie's 25th and last season with the team. It launched a string of seven consecutive non-playoff campaigns, including my last five seasons at the mic.

The personnel of the team in that era left something to be desired. There were players who came into the league after expansion and some of them were good enough to be there, but others were on the fringe. The WHA teams and some of their players, they were good pro hockey players, but they were mediocre compared to the NHL. Some of them gambled on some of those players.

Certainly, Bobby Hull electrified the game throughout western Canada when he went to Winnipeg, but overall, you'd have to say the WHA's presence hurt the NHL because of the damage it did to the talent pool. In 1974-75, my last year of broadcasting, there were 32 teams playing major pro hockey, an all-time high.

It was the same in all sports. I used to go and watch a lot of baseball at Tiger Stadium in the afternoons. I think at one time, I knew every player on both the Tigers and the visiting teams for every team because we'd be there almost every other day, goofing off in the afternoons. Now I've got to get a roster every time a team comes to town to figure out who they are and where they came from. When I started in broadcasting, reasonable ticket prices were available in those days. You could get pretty inexpensive seats for an evening's entertainment. And you got to know the players in every sport. The expansion of hockey, the expansion of baseball, the expansion of football, as a writer or a broadcaster, it's almost impossible to keep up until you get the roster of who's coming in. Fans feel the same way. You're lucky if you can name nine players on every baseball team.

During my last five seasons, the Wings posted just one winning season and won only 144 of 392 games. Take a look at the stats book at the number of coaches they had. Between 1970-77, there were seven coaches. When you take a look at the number of coaches they had, ex-players and ex-Red Wings some of them, it's not difficult to understand why the team struggled. Johnny Wilson came in, but he was viewed as a college coach. Doug Barkley had been a good Red Wing before he got hurt and he was brought in to coach on two different occasions. Ted Garvin lasted just 12 games in 1973-74, literally walking off the job, leaving the bench in the dying moments of a loss to Philadelphia, having already been informed it would be his last game as coach of the club.

It's a terrible thing to say, but people like that just fill the gap. The material on the ice was still the same, but there was a lot of resentment and a lot of non-camaraderie, I guess you'd call it. The attitude of a kid that works for a boss shows in hockey as well. If management has hired a guy to be your coach, he's your coach and you've got to play to his dictate. If you have an objection, go and talk to him.

That wasn't the way it was working during this time frame. Some of them blamed the other guy. "It wasn't my fault that they got through the defense and scored. The goalie should have stopped it. It was an easy shot." Sure, it didn't help that every time you turned around, there was somebody new behind the bench. Losing is very tough on the broadcasters, too. You get close to the personnel, the people who work for the team. You get to know them and their families and you feel sorry for them when it happens.

When things were going haywire, every place you went, there seemed to be an undercurrent. When the team was on the road in those mediocre years, we'd get ahead 4-1 going into the third period, but you've got to have a plan for the final 20 minutes, too. The opposition has picked some of your brain to that stage. They're down three goals, but the fans are with them, and if you can neutralize the top scoring guys, as the visiting teams did to Detroit during those years, nobody could put the puck into the net. It's such a fast sport, speed is important and there are certain coaches who can slow a game down.

During the lean years, when things were down, as a broadcaster I think you think positively. You have to approach it that way to do your job properly. The team would have trained well, had two good days of practice, and go into Montreal, and then they've got to go to Boston and New York afterwards. It's beyond your control as a broadcaster, but in the warm-up, you can almost sense whether there was going to be a little bite to the team or not. The determination to get on the ice, to get ready, and in those days, I think some players didn't want to be in the starting lineup. They wanted to be on the third line. It's a shame because they didn't want to be embarrassed.

The team was going through so many changes at the time, and another major change was afoot following the 1974-75 season. After more than a quarter century at the mic, I decided the time was right to step aside.

Back at the Mic

CHAPTER ELEVEN

❝ *The one that waits the fine day, gets the fine day."*

- Irish Proverb

I decided following the 1974-75 season that it would be a good time to leave my play-by-play duties with the Red Wings. After 25 years in radio and TV, I announced my retirement. Well, sort of. In 1975, that's when longtime Red Wings captain Alex Delvecchio became general manager of the team - he'd been named coach the season before - and asked me to be the club's public relations director. I figured that was a good indication to call it quits, but still be in the Red Wings organization. It's funny, you know, when I think back on the decision. Alex's career as GM didn't last long - he was let go in 1977 - but I was there in the P.R. department until 1985.

It turned out that my broadcasting career wasn't quite done yet. After I left in 1975 to go to work for Alex Delvecchio, Bruce Martyn had Red Wings Hall of Famer and former coach and GM Sid Abel working with

I did play-by-play and Alex Delvecchio provided analysis for ONTV, a subscription service that offered Red Wings games on a pay-per-view basis.

him for awhile, and I got called to pinch-hit for Sid one day because he'd broken his hip in a freak accident at the rink. I remember it well. I'm at home and Bruce Martyn is supposed to be going to Buffalo for the game. Sid's at the rink with his two grandkids, skating after the team's morning practice session, and of all times, Sid forgot to take his skate guards off. He goes on the ice and right up in the air. He broke his hip and he was laid up. Bruce was already airborne to Buffalo. He called me the first chance he could and said, "Catch a plane, you're coming to Buffalo to fill in for Sid Abel, who broke his hip because he didn't know that skate guards don't go on the ice." Poor Sid.

What's amazing to me, when you consider the turnover in broadcasters in today's sports world, is that I only worked with three partners in a quarter-century at the mic. I started with Al Nagler, and Larry Adderley worked briefly one season, and then I worked with Bruce Martyn for 12 years after that. Sometimes on a road trip, an injured player would come up and sit with me, and I'd use him, but basically, you were a loner doing play-by-play on the radio in those days.

After working for years with Sid, Bruce teamed up with former Wing Paul Woods, and he and Paul did a good job. Paul works well with Ken Kal, who followed Bruce into the booth after Bruce retired. If I'm not mistaken, Paul broke his leg in training camp with Montreal one fall and the Canadiens basically gave up on him. I said to him one time, "Couldn't you convince the Canadiens to keep you?" He said, "No." Scotty Bowman got hurt playing junior hockey, and they put a plate in his head. After that, they were always leery of guys with serious injuries. Paul was a short, dapper little guy and he was a real spark plug and fan favorite with the Wings in the late 1970s and early 1980s.

Television is about adding words to the picture, but I really think there's too much talking in televised sports today. I love baseball, but boy, oh boy, those guys have so many stats. And some of our broadcasters in the National Hockey League, they have reams of information, three-by-five cards on every player - where he came from, whether he's married and has kids. A lot of that, if timely enough, can help a broadcast, but I think they overdo it. They should save it once in a while. That's my opinion.

While part of the Wings P.R. staff, I also did some work for the team in the community relations field, making speeches and presentations. That was enjoyable work, but to me, the greatest feeling I've ever gotten from getting out in the community is being able to help those like me who've been forced to deal with the loss of a limb. I go to hospitals all the time. I still do it and will always do it. Our amputee group in Windsor is very active.

I've done this work for years and really never sought to get any publicity for it. It was just a cause that was dear to my heart and something which really mattered to me. Behind the scenes I help others who have suffered a loss similar to mine: Women who have mastectomies, people that have arms off through industrial accidents, even people who have legs off, and kids who get injured in accidents. What I say is simple - get out and be seen. If you have an empty sleeve or a mastectomy or whatever, don't be afraid to be seen. Don't feel shame. If it bothers other people, well, you're not the one with the problem, they are.

I go and see them at the doctor's request or the family's request, but with no publicity. I'd sit with them for awhile and I'd say to them, "Don't be afraid to be seen with an empty pant leg or an empty sleeve. I've been on television, and everybody knows I've only got one arm. It's you yourself that has to adjust. Let other people stare if they want to. They'll ask questions, so have an answer for them."

I guess in the rehabilitation, I've had some very successful things happen. One time, Mike Souchak, who was the head golf pro at Oakland Hills, called me and said, "Budd, we've got a problem." I said, "Now what's up, Mike." And he said, "Mike Edgerton, the greenskeeper at Meadowbrook Country Club, was coming back from the Tigers game the other night and rolled his van and they're trying to sew his arm back on up at the hospital in Ann Arbor."

I waited a couple of days and I called Edgerton up there. I got through to him and I said, "Mike, it's the one-armed bandit." "Mr. Lynch?" he says. "No, Budd," I told him. "I understand that they've made a decision, so I just want you to know that your wife and kids will get used to seeing the empty sleeve, and you'll get used to it. And when you get out of the hospital, I'll come to see you with a golf club. And by the way, the board of directors have rehired you as the greenskeeper." I honestly didn't know whether they did or not. But you know what? He's still there.

This one time, I go out to see Mike. He could shoot in the 90s and I was shooting in the low 90s at the time and a couple of the members of the club, including the club champion – a guy named Breckenreck – and Mike decided he wanted to play them. We got 10 strokes, five each nine. Anyway, we're on the 16th hole, going to the 17th tee, and we've got them nailed. Out from the clubhouse come about 20 guys from the card room. They came out to watch us play the last two holes. Breckenreck stands on the tee and says, "If I lose to these two one-armed SOB's, I'm going to quit the club." He went in after the round and his buddies cleaned his locker out.

A couple of weeks later, I was back at Meadowbrook and made arrangements with Alex Delvecchio, who was in the business of making plaques as a sideline, and I had him make up a special plaque. Sportscaster Ray Lane was a member out there, so I had him make a speech. The plaque read: Meadowbrook Golf and Country Club, July of whatever year it was, Mike Edgerton and Budd Lynch, wingees, defeated Smith and Breckenreck. Very embarrassing to the club members. Know what I had put on the plaque? A single cuff link. Mike still has it in his maintenance shack out there.

Sparky Anderson, when they had the Catch Tournament, he always said, "I've got to get my picture taken with the bookends." That's what they called us, because Mike was missing the left arm and I'm missing the right arm.

We were sitting in the clubhouse one day and I said to Mike, "If I could teach you one more trick: You don't have to lace your shoes every day." At the time, his wife was doing it. "Get slip on shoes," I told him. Velcro was just coming out then. I told him, "Get a hold of a guy in the pro shop to order you some Velcro shoes and charge them to a member's account." He ended up with Velcro even on his work clothes, he got little buckles on them. "Boy this is fast," he'd say. "You can take them off in a hurry, too." Those are some little tricks of the trade that we all learn out of necessity.

I got a call another time. A bartender in Grand River had asked me if I would go and talk to this boy, who had lost his wrist in a meat-cutting accident. And he was going to Michigan State, too. It was a summer employment job. I went to see him - Mike Harrison was his name - and the parents were there, but I said, "I want to talk to Mike by himself." He was about 16 or 17. We were sitting in the kitchen, and his little sister, who was about 11 or 12, was hiding on the stairs. I didn't even know she was listening. I asked him, "What are you worried about right now?" and he said, "I can't play golf." "Sure you can play golf," I told him. "I'll get a friend of mine, Arnold Palmer, to send you some stuff." I had met Arnold at different times, and he did a lot of this type of helpful work behind the scenes, too. Mike, he was on Cloud 9 after I told him that. "You can play golf," I told him again. In fact, we went out on the lawn with my five-iron. He had a whole shoulder and a stump. I said, "You've got control of your whole body. If you concentrate and practice, practice, practice, you'll get it."

We went back inside and I said, "What's that over there on the ceiling?" "Beets soup," he told me. He'd splashed beets up there. I said, "What happened?" He said, "Well, Mr. Lynch, I tried to open two separate cans of beets and it didn't work out very well." I said, "Oh, I'll show you how to do that. Sit on the floor, take the electric can opener and plug it in. Now take the can of beets and put it between your feet. Put the electric can opener down there and when the lid's off, unplug it, take it away, get up and you've got the can of beets open. Put them in the pot." You see, he had to cook a meal in the afternoon for the little girl while their parents were at work. So when they got home that night, guess what the little girl said? "Daddy, look. No more beets on the ceiling."

Anyway, young Mike went to Michigan State. I did the Buick Open its first two years, so I got to know the guys at Warwick Hills and got to know Arnie, Tony Lema and Chi Chi Rodriguez. We would sit around at night and they were interested to know why I would want to play golf with one arm. They kept kidding me all the time. They knew there was a one-armed pro at the time by the name of Jimmy Nicholl. I happened to say to Arnie's agent that there was this kid, who was going to Michigan State and was a pretty good golfer in high school, and he doesn't think he's going to be able to play golf anymore because he's lost his hand and he's got a stump. I got the kid's address at State and Arnold Palmer sent him a five, seven and a nine-iron, a seven-wood, a putter and two dozen golf balls. I'll give him credit. The kid ended up making the golf team.

Everyone has something to give, and I'll help people whenever I can.

Another joy for me over the years has been my golf tournament, the Budd Lynch Celebrity Golf Classic, which benefits the Downriver Guidance Clinic. This year was the 17th year I've done it. My second wife, Thelma, and I lived in Wyandotte, and when they came up with the idea of a guidance center, I wanted to give something back. I volunteered to help, and they came up with the idea of a golf tournament. "We're going to call it the Budd Lynch Celebrity Golf Classic," they told me. "You get the celebrities." I get 30-36 celebrities every year from Red Wings alumni like Johnny Wilson, Bill Gadsby and Gerry Abel; broadcasters like Bruce Martyn, Ray Lane, Art Regner and Devin Scillian; ex-Lions such as Eddie Murray, Dorne Dibble and Horace King; and ex-Tigers including Tom Timmerman, Larry Pashnick and Jeff Kaiser. It's been a real challenge because there are so many outings and so many conflicts. But it's been a labor of love because the guidance center is taking care of needy families, trying to help them readjust when there's alcohol or drugs involved. We hold it at the Grosse Ile Golf & Country Club, and we've got so many great volunteers involved and so many brilliant people helping out. We also run a youth clinic the day of the event, to encourage youngsters to take up the game, which only made sense, since helping kids is what the day is all about. We take in about $70-80,000 every year, but I've never played in it. I'm too busy getting the guys together and making sure everything goes off smoothly.

Not getting out on the course, that's tough for me because I love to golf. I'm a golf nut. I try to play two or three times per week and can usually score in the high 80s or low 90s. I don't go for distance, I just try to hit three solid five-irons and hope for a strong tail wind. Here's a funny story - the last time I played golf with two arms, I shot 101. My first 18 with one arm, I scored 99.

It's been amazing to witness how hockey has grown in Michigan at every level of the game. High school hockey caught on, college hockey became big. It all comes back to the promoting of the sport across the state by the people who ran the Red Wings. The key people in the organization were the ones who sold the sport. Jack Adams always said, "You've got to sell the sport." And it's worked. I'll never forget one time. I was at an Essex Scottish reunion and some guys from Chatham were there. They showed me this picture. We went down to Chatham one time, and it was a hotbed of hockey in its own way. At the banquet that night in Chatham, we brought Steve Yzerman, who was a kid then, in his first year with the team. This one guy came up to me and said, "This is my picture with Stevie from that night. Now I've got to get my grandson in one."

I enjoyed working in the P.R. department. It was a good transition from the broadcast booth, keeping me involved in the game. To me, public relations is basically human relations. It's about dealing with people. It's also a job that cannot be done alone, and I was fortunate to work with wonderful people on the Wings staff like Al Coates, Bill Jamieson, Kathy Best, Morris Moorawnick and Suzy Fontaine.

After 25 years at the mic, then another 10 as P.R. director, it was 1985 and that was the year they put me in the Hockey Hall of Fame with the Foster Hewitt Memorial Award. Gordie Howe was the one who introduced me that night and he turned to me at the podium and said, "Budd, I had to think. Should I give you the award in your left or your right hand?"

When I go up to the Hall of Fame every year, I still see some of the old crowd. It's a thrill in your lifetime to be enshrined with these other people, to be associated with someone like Foster Hewitt, who was a personal friend.

NHL president John Ziegler presented me with this miniature Stanley Cup as a milestone to recognize my long service to the game.

Posing with Wings defenseman Vladimir Konstantinov in the JLA lobby. What a loss it was to the Wings when he suffered a brain injury in a limousine crash shortly after Detroit's 1997 Stanley Cup win.

By this time, the Ilitch family had bought the team and were beginning the turnaround that would bring the franchise back to the top. Mike and Marian Ilitch, they were fans at Olympia and that's when I first met them. After the announcement of my selection to the Hall of Fame, I sent another letter to Mike and Marian Ilitch. It read, "I think I've been around long enough. It's a young man's field and I enjoyed it." They'd given me season tickets, so I was going to be at all the games anyway.

After the ceremonies when I went into the Hall of Fame, I came back to Detroit and the Ilitches had me down to the building, Joe Louis Arena, on a Sunday night. I didn't know why. That's when they threw a surprise party for me with 300 people. All the people who were at the Hall of Fame in Toronto, all of my relatives that I'd said goodbye to there, they brought them there. Coatesey flew in. The Ilitches sent Thelma and I to Hawaii for three weeks. When I went to thank them, that's when Marian said to me, "Mike doesn't like to go out in the public; he doesn't like to give speeches; he doesn't like to go to banquets. So why don't you do some of that for us? Hang around with the community relations people and the public relations department if they need any help." That's when they talked me into doing the public address. "We want you to help out in community relations and do the P.A.," Marian said. And then she added, "Practice until you get it right." What a great line. I'd tried to retire for a second time, but I never really left the atmosphere.

Mike and Marian gave me a plaque that's hanging on the wall at home. It's so thoughtful and it was their thoughts.

I started doing the P.A. in 1985. That's when Bill Jamieson took over as P.R. director. What a hard-working, super guy. He's on our executive board with the golf tournament.

It wasn't long after that when things started to look up again for the franchise. There were conference final appearances in 1987 and 1988, and the club's first Stanley Cup final appearance since 1966 came in 1995. Although it ended in disappointment when the Wings were swept by New Jersey, it was becoming obvious that it was just a matter of time until the Cup came back to Detroit.

That moment finally came in 1997 when the Wings swept Philadelphia, and I was the only one at Joe Louis Arena that night who could say he was also at the mic when the Wings won their previous Cup at Olympia back in 1955. When I had to say, "Last minute of play in this period," I thought about saying, "Last minute of play in this season," but that wouldn't have been appropriate. It was emotional for everyone - the Ilitches, the fans, the captain, Steve Yzerman, who'd probably wondered if he'd ever get to lift that mug. I'll never forget the parade down Woodward Ave. to celebrate the victory. There must have been close to a million people lining the streets. I think all the kids and all the teachers took that day off school. There were two more Stanley Cups after that, in 1998 and 2002, and who knows, there might be another one before long.

The Wings have won 10 Stanley Cups, and I've been there for seven of them. You learn to treasure those special moments. When you think back on your career, the people you meet in all walks of life and certainly as a broadcaster and doing P.A. work the last several years, there are so many lasting memories. I still see a lot of the old players. Some are scouts, some are general managers. They're still in the sport and they're friends, too. The broadcasters you meet, the P.R. people, the people at the league office who were so nice to me over the years. I've been lucky to be around.

I've also been blessed with a wonderful family life.

Seven times, I've been lucky enough to witness the Wings lifting Lord Stanley's mug.

The Lynch Mob

CHAPTER TWELVE

" *It's a pleasure to grow old...many are denied the privilege."*

- Irish Proverb

I've enjoyed a wonderful and fascinating career, but none of my success would possible without the love and support of a wonderful family. And none of it would be worthwhile without loved ones to share it with.

Fortunately, I've been blessed in this regard. Like all families, there have been some rough spots and difficult moments, but I wouldn't trade my life with anyone.

My life didn't start out on the usual plane for a child raised in the 1920s. I grew up as part of a single-parent family. My mom raised the three of us. My sister, Marg, was born in Montreal, and shortly after my dad died in 1919, mom was expecting Edie. Mom continued to work in Hamilton, Ont., at a place called the Right Store, a huge department store. They called her back to work after we moved back to Hamilton.

Mom died at the age of 96. She loved to come down to Detroit to visit us. She was a trooper and she liked to have her cocktails. The Canadian drink in those days was Canadian Club and Coke. She'd have two straws. By the time we picked up our first drink, she'd be down to the bottom of her glass. "Mom," we'd say, "Wait until we get started." And she'd say, "I'm ready for my next one."

People wonder what it was like to grow up without a father in that era. I can understand when a son has a dad with him for most of his life, a real father to a kid, but when you haven't got it, you have uncles who take you under your care. We had relatives in the United States. We had to go to Detroit to visit family, to Hormel, N.Y., and to Chicago. The relatives all wanted to do something for my mom, so they offered to take us three kids over there. One of the breaks in life is that we got to meet a lot more family members than you would have probably met otherwise.

Most of my relatives came from the United States. The ones in New York owned a drug store, another was a doctor and the other uncle in Detroit had a drug store in the Gotham Hotel for years. They always wanted us to move over with them - first my sister Marg and then they wanted me. But mom said, "No, we're staying together." We visited, but we didn't want to pick up roots and become their adopted kids.

It was a different time. Not many had a car in those early days. You had a bike and you walked to school. I walked uptown. Streetcar rides were a big thrill. I remember taking my own family back to Hamilton to show them where I used to live at 32 Fairly Ave. North. Never mind a car, the houses were so close together that between them, there was barely enough room for a bike. The kids said, "Where'd you park the car?" Well, there was an alley, but we didn't have a garage because we didn't have a car. Nowadays, some of these kids are getting cars when they're 16 or 17.

You enjoyed the basics of life and you appreciated it if your health held up. I worked three jobs. I worked on the boats in the summer; I worked part-time in a drug store, and I worked in a hardware store. I guess I was always active that way. I told my mother before she died, I promised to help put my sisters through school, to help them to do what they wanted to do. My one sister Marg went to college to be a beautician and worked at a hotel in Hamilton. Edith, my other sister, wanted to become a nurse, so I provided the funds for her to go through nursing training in Hamilton. I guess that was part of the fatherly instinct that I had acquired. They both went on to be successes in their own right. Edith raised seven children and Marg had one.

I met my first wife, Frances, in Hamilton. I knew her during our school days and we got married just before I went overseas in 1941. I came back to Montreal on assignment and she joined me there. Then we went back to Hamilton and eventually to Windsor, to CKLW. I rented a cottage right near Thomas' Edgewater Inn. That was our first home and that's where Jan, our oldest daughter, was born in Tecumseh. Then we moved up on Hall Ave. All the guys from the service were buying homes up on Ypres Park. They were building these small homes up there like mad, but I moved into an old home, a house that had a big porch with a swing on the porch and a pool table in the basement, of all things. There was a coal chute on the side with a funnel, and the coal would go right down the chute into the fire pot. It was a primitive home, but it was home.

My wife became very sick after the war. She smoked in bed, of all things, and I used to raise hell about it. I smoked cigars, but I would go downstairs into the basement and smoke them in my office. She got to a stage where she was unfortunately hanging around with the wrong type of people in Dearborn. They played bridge three times a week and they couldn't figure out why Budd wasn't there. Well, I was traveling with the hockey team. I was on the go all the time. I also worked radio and TV shows. I had three jobs even then.

She and her sister ganged up on me, and she divorced me. It was a real shock to me and all of the kids. I remember talking to the lawyer and the priest, and the priest said, "She's made her mind up and pardon the expression, she's on the fringe of being suicidal." She had threatened the kids. She said she'd fix me someday. She'd take her own life and take one of the kids with her. That's when the lawyer and the doctor and the priest all said that you've got to give in to her. She won't listen to reason. She's listening to her Canadian relatives instead of listening to the people she should be listening to.

We went to counseling and the one counselor we saw was very good. Fran wouldn't let me drive her there, she said she'd find her own way there. Well, she got lost and showed up a half an hour late. As soon as she walked in, she said to the counselor, "Well, he's been here telling all kinds of lies about me, so I'm not going to stay." She'd made her mind up, I guess. She moved back to Canada after the divorce. I saw her quite a bit afterwards. We kept in touch until she passed away. I provided money for the kids because they were with her up there.

Later, it came out, that she never wanted to move to the States. She wanted to stay close to her family to Chatham. She resented from Day 1 that we had come over to the States. Later on in life, she told the kids this. She thought I should have stayed in Canada. I was a Canadian. I was an officer in the Essex Scottish. I worked in radio and had a good job. I should have stayed there. It was one of those things, I guess, but time marches on.

I had no desire to ever get married again. When Fran passed away, by a quirk of fate in 1976, I ended up playing golf and meeting the woman who would become my second wife, at a golf tournament. At that time, I was a member at the Grosse Ile Golf and Country Club. I played in the invitational, and one of the group's playing partners couldn't come in from Chicago that year, so some friends of mine, Sonny and Marilyn Gandee, they asked me to play. I was playing to 89-93, in that bracket, so I was creditable. I ended up playing in the tournament and there was a dinner and dance on Saturday night, so my playing partners said to me, "You've got to get a date." I said, "I'm not dating anybody. I don't want to go to a dance." So Marilyn, one of our group, lined up Thelma Pruske. She worked for the city of Wyandotte, and she called her at her apartment and said, "Budd would like to take you to the dinner-dance on Saturday night." Marilyn came back and said, "Yes, she'd like to go, but she doesn't know who you are, though." And I said, "Well, that's good." To make a long story short, I got a bottle of wine and went over to her apartment. She played golf at West Shore, and she'd played in the invitational at Grosse Ile, so she knew golf. She asked me, "Do you ever play West Shore?" And I said, "Two or three times a month. A lot of the Red Wings go up there, and Normie Smith is a member." She said, "I've never seen a one-armed guy play golf." So I said, "You're going to have a surprise then someday." The final day of the golf tournament, we weren't playing for the title, we were coming in second and she came out and followed us for the last three holes. She said, "Are you sure you've played West Shore? How come I've never seen a one-armed guy out there?" I said, "You women are all either playing cards, drinking beer or playing golf. You didn't want the men around, so you never notice us."

So we hit it off and dated for about three or four years. She had no

Thelma and I join Ed and Nancy Tuinier in the Grosse Isle Country Club clubhouse during my charity golf tournament in 1989.

family because her husband had died. She knew I had six daughters and she'd met five of them by this time. The sixth one, the baby, Lori, was living in San Diego. She said to me, "If you're thinking about getting married, then I've got to meet that baby first." So I got two airplane tickets for us to fly out to San Diego. It turned out to be a good move. Lori was so pleased to meet her. I got up one morning and they were in the garage talking. Lori was doing her laundry, so I decided to go for a walk. I figured they'd either end up killing each other or they're going to get along. I came back after a couple of pops and I could hear them laughing like hell. I stuck my nose in and said, "Everything alright?" And they said, "Where the hell have you been?" I said, "I was at a bar." So they said, "Go back to the bar. We're still busy talking." So I went down the street to another bar and came back in an hour.

We got married the next fall, by ourselves. I told the girls by wire that I was getting married. I didn't say whether it was morning or afternoon, and I didn't say where. Two of the smart girls called every hotel to try and find out where we were registered, but I was registered under an assumed name. We were going to London, Ont., where I'd been in the army, and that's where we stayed on our honeymoon. We stayed for three days and even got in a little golf. The kids were so funny. They said, "We've got to get you back."

The girls were always the inquisitive sort. None of them ever played hockey, but they all brought boys home who were looking to get their hands on some Red Wings tickets. While in school in 1949, we had three kids and another on the way, and Jan, the oldest, came home from school one day, and said, "The teachers at Divine Child know who you are, and they want you to come in and give a talk to the kids." And then she added, "Well Dad, I've got a question to ask. One kid that I'm very close to in school, she wants to know why we don't have one-armed babies?" I told her the order was never put in that way.

The year the Wings won the Cup in 1997 with Mike Vernon as the goalie, after the final game of the series was over, he came over to the Alumni Club where the alumni would gather, and he gave Thelma the goalie stick he'd used in the game, autographed. We'd taken him out to dinner a couple of times and become friends. The P.R. director from the Hockey Hall of

Fame, he called me and asked, "Have you got Vernon's stick from the championship game?" and I said, "No, my wife has it." So Vernon had to sign another hockey stick to give to the Hall of Fame. The original is still in my basement. One of my grandkids is heir to it.

My grandkids are not hockey players. They're soccer players, baseball players, two of them are golfers, so I told them, "One day I'm going to hold a drawing and whoever holds the lucky number is going to get all of my hockey lore." Including the Vernon stick.

Thelma used to joke that we took so long to get married because I had the six daughters from my first marriage. She would shake her head and ask, "How can anyone get along with six other females?" But she did, and they all adored her.

Thelma handled those kids like they were her own, and they thought the world of her, which was so nice. When she became sick - she had two strokes - they went out of their way to do whatever they could for her. You don't realize what a stroke does to a person. Their brain power is still there, but they're limited in what they can do. Our daughters visited her at the hospital, they visited her at home. It augured well that I'd made a choice like that because we were so compatible and we had so much in common. And then to have your own family accepted by a person who didn't have a family, it gave good piece of mind to me.

We lost Thelma on March 8, 2003, two months before what would have been our 20th wedding anniversary. She was 77. She had suffered a series of strokes and had battled cancer. The ticker just gave out and she peacefully slipped away. She worked for 47 years in the Wyandotte Municipal Services Department and; like me, she just couldn't seem to retire. Twice she tried, but both times they called her back to work. She became a really big Red Wings fan and the Ilitch family gave her season tickets so that she could attend every game. She got to know all of the players and their families. She loved the sound of bagpipes, so at the funeral, I had a bagpiper come to mass to pipe her into heaven.

We never know why we're here or how long we're going to be here, but what I do know is that life has to go on. I've learned over the years that if you do things for other people, you will receive so much love and warmth in return.

I've been lucky to have a family that shares the same beliefs. My six daughters - Janis Ruffino, Valerie Morris, Mary Schimizzi, Frances Lary, Patricia Lamerato and Lori Zilstra, their husbands and eight grandchildren are all wonderful, loving, caring people.

Jan, Valerie and Mary were born in Windsor, and Frances, Patricia and Lori were born in Dearborn. Every girl had an education. They all started in college. Some finished and some didn't. Jan graduated from Michigan State, became a teacher and later moved to Chicago with her husband. They ended up settling in Wilmot, Ill., up near Libertyville, not far from Norris's place. She's retired now and they live in Huntley, Ill., near Chicago. Val lives in Allen Park; Mary lives in Novi; Francie lives in Livonia; and Patty lives in Northville. Lori is in San Diego.

Frances, Patty and Val all went to dental school, and Frances still works in a dentist's office. Lori runs her own business in San Diego. She's a CPA handling books for lawyers and doctors. She's done very well for herself. Mary works for her husband, who has a para-medical legal operation.

Of the eight grandchildren, Caroline works in a plumbing office in East Detroit. Joe Schmizzi, Mary's son, he was an all-state soccer player, but when he went to Michigan State, he didn't want to play soccer, so he taught soccer and coached the women's soccer team at Michigan State. Joe married Kendra and they now have a son. The Lamerato's daughter Stephanie is now at MSU, and Anton, he's confided in his parents and told me he wants to join the Marine Corps. Out in California, Lori has a boy, Nicholas, he's just eight and he's into everything from soccer to stickball.

When I talk about family, I often think about all of the women who were part of the broadcasting team who helped me, people like Kathy Best. Everybody who worked at Olympia Stadium and then at the Joe, these were dedicated people. The nice thing about it, too, is that we used to get together every year, right across from Port Huron on the Lake Huron side, there's a hangout there. Not a resort area, but they've got a golf course. We'd take the gang up there and the employees would bring their spouses. We'd play golf and after, Kathy Best's husband, Al, and Ruth Hoffman – who worked in the building – her husband, Al, and Marilyn Charbonneau's husband, Wilf, would arrive for cocktail hour. And they all had the right sleeve of their shirts tucked in to mimic me. So I made each of them keep it that way for one hour. I said, "You're going to learn to make a drink left-handed, to get the cookies ready, get the food ready, you're not going to move that other arm at all." Well, their left arms were so tired after that hour; they were begging me to let them get their right arms back. "You dirty old man," they said.

That's the beautiful thing about spending a life in hockey. The people in this game are truly one big, happy family. I'm always thankful to have worked with so many loyal, dedicated Red Wings personnel. It's been a privilege to work under two owners, the Norris and Ilitch families. I'll never forget the tribute Mike and Marian Ilitch paid to me after my induction into the Hockey Hall of Fame. Likewise, I'll always be moved by the memories I've shared and continue to share with my close friends Bruce Marytn and Sonny Eliot. I'm still touched when I think of Bruce's glowing speech that he made as he introduced me upon my induction into the Michigan Sports Hall of Fame. I was also enshrined in the Windsor/Essex County Sports Hall of Fame, and it's a special feeling when your hometown recognizes you.

Over the years, I've treasured the many long-term bonds I've formed with fans, many of whom traveled with us from Olympia Stadium to Joe Louis Arena. I'm thrilled to have been given the opportunity to give back to the community that has embraced me so warmly, working to help amputees face life and playing host to my golf tournament, raising funds for those less fortunate.

Working as the public address announcer at Red Wings home games and college games at Joe Louis Arena has allowed me to keep in touch with many of the players whose careers I followed as a broadcaster, some of whom have stayed in the game as coaches, general managers and scouts. And I've formed lasting personal relationships with so many hockey media people, NHL broadcasters, writers, photographers, league personnel and team P.R. directors. It's been a pleasure coming to the rink every day.

I've been with the Red Wings for 57 years and never scored a goal. I've never paid to see a hockey game, either. And I've got no plans to stop coming and doing my job because I don't know how anyone could have more fun and still have someone call it work.

So you can count on seeing me at the rink and hearing me over the sound system. If my career shows anything, it's this - as long as the voice holds up, I guess you can hang around.